Despite nearly being killed by a kangaroo and almost lynched
and run out of town after his comedy was taken far too seriously, Sami Shah is very happy to be living in Australia. He
has fronted his own satirical show on television in Karachi,
worked as a journalist, and been a highly regarded newspaper
columnist – all dangerous occupations to be involved in – when
the combination of seeing the aftermaths of a devastating
bomb attack and being the target of death threats convinced
him to leave Pakistan. Under the terms of their Australian
migration visa, Sami and his wife and young daughter were
obliged to settle in a rural area, and so they moved to Northam
in Western Australia.

Now Sami is battling a crippling addiction to meat pies,
but at least is no longer constantly mistaken for an escaped
asylum seeker from the nearby detention centre. He has also
been the star of *Australian Story*, the subject of an article in the
New York Times, and has performed countless comedy shows
to ever-growing and appreciative audiences.

I, MIGRANT

A COMEDIAN'S JOURNEY FROM KARACHI TO THE OUTBACK

SAMI SHAH

ALLEN&UNWIN
SYDNEY•MELBOURNE•AUCKLAND•LONDON

First published in 2014

Allen & Unwin
83 Alexander Street
Crows Nest NSW 2065
Australia
Phone: (61 2) 8425 0100
Email: info@allenandunwin.com
Web: www.allenandunwin.com

Cataloguing-in-Publication details are available
from the National Library of Australia
www.trove.nla.gov.au

ISBN 978 1 74331 934 5

Set in 11.75/17.5 pt Chaparral Pro by Bookhouse, Sydney
Printed and bound in Australia by Griffin Press

10 9 8 7 6 5 4 3 2 1

FOR ISHMA

FOR MOMMY AND DADDY

AND, ALWAYS, FOR ANYA

PROLOGUE

I saw my first kangaroo ten months after moving to Australia. Or, to be more accurate, I saw my first *live* kangaroo.

I had previously seen many dead kangaroos as I drove along the Great Eastern Highway, a vast curving stretch of blacktop connecting Perth to the town of Northam. Their bodies littered the side of the road, issuing reminders of the speed limit in a grisly mess of twisted necks and spilled intestines. I've always wondered how they managed to get to the roadside so quickly, some of the corpses still bleeding when I passed. Is a driver who rams one legally required to get out of the car and pull the wrecked marsupial out of the way? Or do they always just bounce sideways conveniently when struck by the front end of a vehicle barrelling along at 110 kilometres an hour? If I was a kangaroo, I'd lie down dead exactly where I was hit and become a large fleshy speed bump over which other cars would hurtle. Fuck the humans.

All the victims of intrastate traffic I'd seen up to then had been quite small, probably no more than four feet tall, but the first live kangaroo I saw was easily over five foot, a massive grey-brown beast that looked like a velociraptor covered in suede. At that size they can be quite a marvellous sight – gargantuan thighs, shoulders and arms as disproportionately muscled as a Russian Olympic weightlifter, and a thick serpentine tail.

Unfortunately, I saw the kangaroo just as I came around a bend, doing 100 kilometres an hour. My headlights stamped it out in the middle of the road; it didn't so much bound into my path as appear suddenly from nowhere, a demon ghost kangaroo burped out by the spirit of Australia to kill me.

I was returning from a gig in Perth and this was the second strange thing to happen to me on the drive home that night. The first had taken place at a petrol station in Sawyers Valley, a dust-mote-sized town laid out like a suburban parenthesis at the start of the Great Eastern Highway. The drive from Perth to Northam takes an hour and a half and, since I leave for most gigs too early to eat dinner and return too late even for drive-thru, my car is usually filled with chocolate wrappers and empty water bottles by the time I reach home. This particular night, wanting to fuel up on snacks, I stopped at the neon-lit pump and walked into the shop attached, hungry for my Snickers.

'You're Sami Shah,' said the man behind the counter, his accent instantly recognisable as Pakistani.

'Yes, yes I am,' I replied. Then, switching to our native Urdu, I asked, 'How did you know?'

'Guess,' he said.

Being recognised is fun. Being made to guess how is not.

'Are you from Karachi as well?' I hazarded. If so he might recognise me from the meagre amount of notoriety I had gained there as an opinion columnist writing for an English daily. Whenever anyone recognised me in Karachi, it was from the terribly smug photograph printed next to my weekly columns, in which I looked straight over my spectacles at the reader with a finger curled over my chin thoughtfully.

It was pretentious and rendered me eminently punchable. When I submitted it, I thought it would be funny. By the second week, even I was sick of the joke.

'No, I'm from Quetta,' he said.

'Then I've got no idea.'

He grinned and reached under the counter for a copy of the freshly delivered Sunday paper. Inside, glaring out above a half-page article, was my photograph.

A PAKISTANI MIGRANT WALKS INTO TOWN, the headline blared.

'This is great!' I thought.

I took a copy, along with a promotional-deal Snickers long enough for Archimedes to shift the world with, and set off, racing towards the kangaroo waiting in my immediate future.

Afterwards, standing in front of my smashed car, the attending policeman told me, 'You shoulda hit the fakking thing. You shoulda just hit the fakking thing.' But all I could think was, 'No I couldn't. I'm an immigrant and I don't think it'd look very good if I'd killed your national emblem.' It seemed like the sort of thing that might come up in my citizenship exam later.

I had swerved, reflexes jerking the steering wheel as soon as I saw the kangaroo, then I'd swerved again to avoid smashing into a tree. My small red Daihatsu Sirion skidded in a gravel patch, spun twice, then flipped. It glided through the air upside down, despite having all the aerodynamism of a 1970s electric razor. The seatbelt defiantly held me in place, even when the roof of the car slapped down onto the asphalt and careened forward in a shower of sparks. The only thing louder than the Japanese hatchback scraping across an Australian highway on its roof was the Pakistani comedian screaming inside.

After several seconds, we came to a stop. I was still strapped to my seat, upside down. I remember saying 'Oh fuck' a lot. Repeating it over and over as I fumbled for the clasp that would release me.

'Oh fuck oh fuck oh fuck.'

Then, when I pressed it and fell on my head, 'Ow fuck.'

The door on the driver's side was punched in and lying on the ceiling of the car. I kicked at it, but it didn't give. Feeling around, I found my spectacles, which were miraculously unbroken. Able to see properly now, I realised the window on the passenger side had completely blown out. I belly-crawled through the gap and onto the cold black road, glass crunching beneath my hands.

'Oh fuck oh fuck oh fuck.'

Once I had extricated myself fully, I stood up and conducted an inspection, rubbing my hands through my hair, across my face and then down over my body. No blood, no cuts and gashes, nothing but a scratch on my right hand where a sliver of gravel had pierced the skin.

'Oh . . . God?'

Nothing challenges an avowed atheist like a miracle.

People stopped. Someone gave me water. Someone else found my cigarettes lying in the middle of the road – another miracle.

The car had to be pulled upright by a tow truck and looked very much like a squashed cupcake. Finally, once the policeman was satisfied that I was neither drunk nor driving an unregistered vehicle, I called a friend and asked for a lift home.

'Don't tell Ishma,' I told the friend, 'She'll be asleep and she has Anya with her and I don't need them panicking. I'll wake her up myself when I get home and she can see I'm fine.'

Half an hour of shivering, caused by both the mid-May chill and being in a mild state of shock, and then the friend arrived and drove me home.

The kangaroo, in case you're worried, survived unhurt. I never saw it again. Some nights, though, I know it's still out there, waiting. We will meet again. I will know him by the scar across his eye and the words GOOD ON YA tattooed across his knuckles. One shall stand and one shall fall.

'Did you think you were going to die?' my friend asked as we finally pulled into Northam.

'Yeah, for a second there I did,' I replied.

'What was that like?'

I considered this for a few seconds, inspecting the tiny scar on my palm as I relived sailing through the air upside down in a car.

Something happens to me in moments of trauma. It's happened before – once when I was standing in the aftermath of a suicide blast, the street littered with human debris, and another time when I had a gun pushed against my temple. A part of my rational thinking mind separates from my body and hovers a few feet above me. Its thoughts are remarkably coherent, if a bit absurd, like an ancestral ghost full of sarcastic wisdom.

I said, 'I thought, "I'm from Karachi. I've survived death by suicide bombing and death by gun. What the hell am I doing in Australia dying by kangaroo?"'

I, JOURNALIST

1

I was just wrapping up my night shift as panel producer at Dawn News when the news director called a meeting. Ideally, I would have liked to go home and catch a nap first, but regular sleep schedules are a luxury rarely afforded in Pakistani journalism.

Since the channel had launched five months before, I was one of three panel producers working eight-hour shifts that rotated every two weeks. The job of a panel producer, on paper, is to produce the news bulletin, to give the anchor the scripts, and to make sure the bulletin airs on time and that all the stories run in a coherent sequence. On paper it sounds quite efficient and systematic and orderly. Whenever they show panel producers in films and TV shows, he's the guy with a microphone stapled to the side of his head, standing in front of a bank of screens, usually wearing a waistcoat, calmly saying things like, 'Cut to camera two!' and 'Fade in three. Two. One.'

In reality, however, the panel producer is more like an octopus with all eight tentacles spearing out at the same time, most of them instantly getting knotted. There are anchor scripts to organise, reporters to connect to, studio cameras to focus and switch between, guests to line up, anchor egos to balance and decisions to make in less time than a brain can process a muscle twitch. You do it all while standing in a darkened room lit only by the urgent flickering of a dozen video monitors. One hand wields a computer mouse as if it were a field surgeon's scalpel being used to slice through innards while under heavy fire, the other taps across a switchboard that offers a selection of camera angles of the news studio and the various streams of footage illuminating the monitors in front of you.

All this is done while receiving instructions from the news director or desk editor through headphones, paying attention to what the anchor is saying on air, providing instructions to whomever you have handling the audio mixing console and graphics machines, and unleashing an incoherent stream of cursing and tortured screams into the microphone hovering half an inch from your mouth:

'Where's the fucking OC for the package on floods? Why is the fucking sound cutting there? There, fuck you . . . fuck fucking fuck . . . There! Cut to this, where I am pointing. Look where I'm pointing – not *you*! Just stay on script when I say cue . . . Cue – yes I just said cue. No, sir, I said cue. And he's still quiet because he's got the brains of an ant. Cut to three! Three!!! Did I say two? I said three, on my cue in three . . . Two, I said fucking cut to three. When I count from three . . .' And so on, for fifty-five minutes until the bulletin ends. Which then gives you exactly three minutes either to drain your bladder, smoke a cigarette or rethink your life choices. Then two minutes of reading through the headlines to catch any mistakes that the plodding editors in the newsroom invariably missed and then the whole thing starts again. For eight hours. Panel producers quickly learn the importance of wearing shoes that are comfortable for standing in, exactly how long it takes to pee or catch a smoke, and to ignore the bursts of tension pain studded through their shoulders and neck.

If you manage to do all of this well, then the viewer at home sees a placid, smiling anchor delivering the latest headlines in measured tones while seamlessly transitioning between stories of bomb blasts in Quetta and two-headed kittens in Texas. If it goes badly, then . . . Well, just do a YouTube search for 'anchor meltdowns'. The regional Fox News anchor who's pelting the camera with papers and curse words is probably doing that because the panel producer wasn't able to contain the chaos.

Rotating the panel producers so that they aren't trapped in the same shift is one way of preventing nervous breakdowns. Each day was divided into three shifts: 8 am to 4 pm, 4 pm to midnight, and midnight to 8 am. The 4 pm to midnight shift was the most intense, leaving everyone involved with smashed nerves and violent nightmares that could only be overcome with years of therapy and medication. Most suicide bombings occur during those hours; it's when politicians swerve into areas of controversy; even earthquakes and tsunamis wait until early evening to wreck your carefully organised bulletin.

The overnight shift, by comparison, can be absolutely soporific. Past midnight, hardly anyone is watching, so even the most urgent of events can be ignored until a cigarette is fully smoked or a quick game of table tennis completed. There is still the odd mad panic of breaking news, but standards can be slackened, safe in the knowledge that the entire viewing audience is asleep. Panel producers hate the overnight shift because in those two weeks their reflexes calcify.

Which is probably why, when the news director called a meeting this particular morning at 8 am, just when my shift was ending, I thought it was to publicly scold me for letting the anchor do the entire 2 am bulletin with a cigarette perched behind one ear.

I walked into the main newsroom, a large space cluttered with desks, computers, camera tripods, journalists and editors. A column of screens on the far wall continuously showed international and local news channels. The news director was standing in front of them, commanding the attention of everyone in the room. A balding man who could turn even the most jaded reporter into a puddle of urine with a glare, Azhar Abbas was the hidden force behind Pakistan's TV news industry. A few years before, he had put the first twenty-four-hour news channel in Pakistan – Geo News – on air and he was now responsible for doing the same for Pakistan's first English news channel, Dawn News. When, a year later, he would leave our channel to return to Geo, the significant drop in quality resulted in Dawn News becoming just another number on the TV remote. After a desperate overhaul, it became known for sensationalist onslaughts and hungry rakings of the bottom of the moral barrel.

Assembled in front of him was every reporter, producer, editor and cameraman working at Dawn News's Karachi office at the time, around fifty men and women all buzzing with anticipation. What I had forgotten was that it was 17 October 2007 and former prime minister Benazir Bhutto was returning to Pakistan after eight years of self-imposed exile. Her plane was due to land in Karachi the next morning. Her political party, the Pakistan People's Party, was going to fill the streets with a million supporters. Every news channel in the world would be there and we needed to organise our coverage, otherwise we'd be lost in the avalanche of breaking news that was bound to happen.

On a whiteboard, Azhar Abbas had drawn a map that showed the route she would take from the airport to where she would deliver a speech in front of the mausoleum built to honour the nation's founder. Along the way, marked out like snipers' nests, were the positions each two-man team (a reporter and a cameraman) would take to get the best coverage.

'Sami,' said Azhar, stabbing at the giant rectangle marked AIRPORT, 'that's going to be you. Three cameramen, two reporters and you in an OB van.'

An Outside Broadcasting van is a large truck with an air-conditioned interior complete with all the technological trappings needed to serve as a mobile news studio. It has a satellite dish attached to the roof to broadcast live footage from multiple cameras, all controlled by a wall of monitors and an array of knobs and switches that the panel producer plays like a virtuoso pianist.

'We got an OB van?' I asked, excited. I didn't know the channel had bought one.

'It's a rental,' said Azhar, 'Don't break it or it comes out of your salary.'

'Yes, sir,' I said. 'I'll go home, grab a nap and then head for the airport.'

'No time. The other news channels will have their teams there already, staking out the best spots. Go now and stay there until tomorrow.'

I'd have argued for a shower at least, but Azhar had already fixed his basilisk glare on me and all protest evaporated. The briefing ended an hour later, after which I grabbed a Red Bull, three cameramen and two reporters, and headed out to see the OB van. I had heard some of the other channels had recently purchased vans of their own. By this time, Pakistan had about as many news channels as there were people to watch them and OB vans were the latest steroid boost in the race to deliver breaking news. Some of the vans used by competing channels were behemoths – anti-tank personnel carriers large enough to block entire streets and fitted out with comforts the like of which a producer could only dream. I was hoping for, at least, an ensuite toilet and air conditioning. Instead, I walked out to the car park to find a small Suzuki ute, its open back filled with TVs piled on top of a nest of cables, circuitry and a satellite dish lying on its back.

'Look!' said the technician. 'We even got a roof for you to stay cool under.' He was carrying a filthy grey carpet that could be held aloft by the four iron rods attached to its ends.

By the time we reached the airport, after stopping to stock up on food, water and more energy drinks, it was late evening. On normal days, Karachi traffic can swallow chunks of time in large gridlock-sized bites. Given the added security measures now being put into place in anticipation of the crowds – barriers arbitrarily narrowing roads, police mobiles blocking popular routes, shipping containers turning thoroughfares into dead-ends and funnelling you through narrow side streets that meandered through convoluted suburban neighbourhoods and then somehow spat you back out exactly where you first started – it took us several hours to reach our destination. But even then, we managed to pull into the airport car park before any of the other news channels. As the sun buried itself under shovelfuls of exhaust-grey clouds, my team and I picked out the best spots, even managing to get one cameraman up on top of a nearby office roof. By the time the other channels got there in their shiny new trucks, we had staked out all the prime journalistic real estate.

--------- • ---------

The next morning, just after the first call to prayer had finished echoing through the city, people started to arrive. A PPP politician roamed the airport grounds, stopping at each channel's setup to record a statement on the historical importance of the event while trying his best to look photogenic.

By the time Benazir Bhutto's plane landed – shortly after midday – the sun-baked car park was congested with ecstatic PPP loyalists. I sat under my drooping carpet in the van's rear; my TV monitors showed men adorned with party flags and posters, looking like political peacocks in full mating glory as they danced hysterically.

We had hired a security guard to keep crowds away from our satellite dish, since it was not placed on the roof of an immovable truck but was resting on the ground next to the van. He managed to stop anyone from interfering with its operation but was unable to keep out the scores of children who clambered into the van and sat crowded around me, providing me with their editorial input.

Our prime camera positions paid off with exclusive footage of Benazir Bhutto disembarking from her plane. While all the other channels had only grainy shots of a distant figure descending onto the tarmac, Dawn News had a close-up of the PPP leader and former prime minister, dressed in the colours of the Pakistani flag, wiping tears from her eyes as she looked up and whispered a prayer of thanks. Even Azhar Abbas was happy with that one.

Benazir Bhutto left the airport on a bus that had been specially built for her security; as high as a double-decker and covered in black bullet-proof metal, it featured a platform on the roof from which she could wave to the adoring crowds, and a private room inside where she could recuperate from waving to the adoring crowds. I imagine you can only stomach the sight of so many grown men wearing garlands around their necks and your picture glued to their chests before needing a bit of a lie-down.

There were thousands of fans inside the airport and over a million more lining the road to her eventual destination, so her bus could only move at a crippled snail's pace, taking close to two hours just to cross the 200 metres of road directly in front of me. Security personnel had given up any effort to clear the route due to the sheer impossibility of the task. Every time Benazir Bhutto emerged on top of her bus and offered the crowds a wave, they would greet her with an hysteria that would make both the Pope and Justin Bieber jealous.

Meanwhile, sitting in a deepening pool of my own sweat that threatened to short-circuit the monitors and electrocute me and my newly acquired battalion of under-age editors, I was grateful when Azhar called to say I had got enough footage from that area and should relocate to the mausoleum. Benazir's bus had lumbered out onto the road and the crowds followed, leaving crumpled posters and crushed garlands in their wake. Thanks to her slow progress, if we stuck to back roads and circled the entire city, we would still make it to the venue hours before her procession arrived. The nap I took while the driver sped across Karachi was the first sleep I'd had in two days.

--------- • ---------

The mausoleum is a white marble building, inside which the man who created Pakistan – Muhammad Ali Jinnah – is entombed. No one is quite sure why the building is modelled on a hard-boiled egg in an eggcup. It's so rarely visited that its grounds are used mainly for secret dating and surreptitious hand jobs, except when politicians needing an impressive backdrop for their pronouncements shoo away the discreetly horny.

When we arrived, the roads around the mausoleum were still relatively deserted. Most of the people milling about were policemen and journalists, buying snacks from roadside vendors and swapping predictions about when the procession would arrive. A Sky News reporter was using a briefcase-sized computer setup to sporadically file pixelated reports, and a BBC crew were chatting with their CNN counterparts. These were being circled by Pakistani reporters, hoping to slip business cards and résumés into the conversation.

We arranged our cameras so our reporter was framed against the eggcup, and then we sat down and waited.

Several hours passed, with our reporter providing short updates about the situation at the mausoleum to the main bulletin. Mostly, we took it in turns to catch up on our sleep – which is what I was doing when my phone rang.

I had managed to drift off into fairly deep unconsciousness while sitting in the Suzuki ute's passenger seat. As I fumbled to pull my phone out of my pocket, I realised mine wasn't the only one ringing. Around me, every reporter from every news channel was responding to the insistent trilling of their own mobile phone. We all saw our respective news director's name flashing on the screen and exchanged glances before simultaneously pressing the answer button. Every one of us knew what we were about to be told.

That there would be a suicide attack on Benazir Bhutto's convoy was, in retrospect, inevitable. It was moving too slowly through crowds packed too tightly for security to be maintained. And this was Benazir Bhutto – the former prime minister of Pakistan, the first and only female leader of a Muslim country, returning to take power from a military dictator while making bold verbal assaults on the Taliban and Al-Qaeda menace that had begun wreaking havoc on the whole nation over the last few months.

We all knew there would be an attack; most of us just assumed it would happen during her speech. Even as Azhar Abbas was telling me there had been two explosions beside the bus carrying Benazir Bhutto, I was frantically motioning for the camera crew and reporters to pile into their cars.

'Aftab was there,' Azhar said. 'He isn't answering his phone.'

Aftab Borka was a reporter who had been at Dawn News since its earliest days, and he had distinguished himself as an excellent journalist. We knew each other well and I instantly went into a deep panic, the kind that doesn't exhibit itself as wild mania but settles heavily against the base of your spine. It wasn't just born of the possibility that Aftab might be dead, although that was obviously worrying. It also came from the fact that I had never been to a bombsite.

Almost my entire time in news so far had been spent safely ensconced in a control room. I had driven through the aftermath of the odd riot or gang war, just as most people in Karachi have at some point, but never a suicide blast. I had an idea of what to expect from editing the footage sent back to us by cameramen in the field. Shots of limbs strewn across roads, their torn ends still bloody; cars crushed like cans by the impact of the blast; craters rimmed with hair and skin. But to see it without the protective distance of a monitor was something I wasn't sure I was prepared for.

'Do your job,' I told myself. 'You were trained for these situations. Do your job.'

I dialled Aftab Borka's number and heard it ring out.

'I don't want to see this,' I thought. 'I don't know if I can handle it.'

'Check your batteries and lights,' I told the cameraman perched on the open back of the ute. Then I dialled Aftab again.

Still no response.

'He's dead,' I thought. 'He died in a suicide blast, and I'm going to have to find his body.'

'Azhar called,' the cameraman shouted through the window. 'He said to keep your phone line free and not to take any footage of body parts.'

'Yeah, keep it clean,' I yelled back at him over the squeal of tyres as we rounded a corner. 'No time to edit it for the bulletin.'

An ambulance screamed past us. Then another. We braked just in time to avoid colliding with a police van going the wrong way. In the distance I could see the oscillating splashes of emergency vehicle lights clustered around what must be the site of the blast.

My hand was shaking and I had some trouble redialling Aftab's number. Then I remembered Azhar Abbas's admonition and hastily ended the call.

'Okay,' I thought, 'I can do this. Besides,' I told myself, with a flash of the dark humour characteristic to Pakistanis, 'it's still better than working in fucking advertising.'

The ute shuddered to a halt. I opened the door and stepped out into carnage.

2

Working in advertising is what drove me to news. Neither had been part of The Plan. The Plan is the grand design for your life that you lay out as a teenager. For some it's becoming a doctor, for others maybe a lawyer, or a musician or, if you are particularly lacking in ambition and are borderline sociopathic, a banker. For me, growing up, The Plan had been to become a writer. I would write Pakistan's first science fiction novel and it would debut on the *New York Times* bestseller list.

Unfortunately, my Plan – like the Plans of most people – was not easily attainable. Inevitably, I was waylaid by The Practical Considerations of Daily Life. Not as catchy as The Plan, but more likely to provide living wages.

The necessity of a change in direction hit me around the time I was graduating from college in America with a degree in English. I had spent four years at the University of Virginia, and wrote a book in a white heat of two weeks during the summer after I graduated. It was a terrible novel, with a plotline that meandered more aimlessly than Karachi's side streets. A cousin let me stay in his apartment while I tried to sell it, but after the tenth rejection letter I realised it might take a little longer than anticipated to achieve my goals.

So I moved to Northern Virginia in search of a job. I soon discovered the world wasn't exactly holding doors open in wait for English majors. And, to be fair, I wasn't trying very hard either, because I had friends in Pakistan telling me about how great it was back there. At that point, Pakistan was in the early stages of what I like to describe as 'The Great Peace and Prosperity Scare of 2002–2006'. Pervez Musharraf had declared himself President-General-Dictator in 1999 and had somehow buoyed Pakistan into a place of economic fertility. That he had managed this in a post-9/11 world, when America was waging war right next door in Afghanistan, was nothing short of a miracle. Every day, I would open my email to find job rejection letters countered by enticing descriptions of creative enterprises that were being richly compensated in Karachi.

So in December 2002, six months after graduating college, I went home. It was my first time back in two years and, whereas previous trips had been short vacations during the summer breaks, this time I had booked a one-way ticket. I still had several months left on my American visa and so I formulated a New Plan: if I didn't get a job in Karachi in three months, I'd go back to the US and keep trying there. Two months after I landed, I started working at an ad agency.

The only reason I took the job as a junior art director at J. Walter Thompson was because their office was awesome. Located right next to a five-star hotel, across the street from a gorgeous colonial-era Venetian-style building and just up the road from the heavily bunkered US consulate, the agency was housed on the top floor of a horseshoe-shaped building made entirely of glass. The first three floors belonged to a bank and you could stand in front of one of the interior glass walls and look down right into the offices below. I often fantasised about throwing a mannequin off the top floor and screaming 'OH MY GOD! HE JUMPED!' as it plummeted past the bankers below.

I first went there to visit a friend who had recently got a job as a copywriter. Waiting in reception, I watched as employees walked up to the front door, pressed their palms into a hand scanner and then entered as the door unlocked automatically.

'It's like freakin' *Mission Impossible*,' I told my friend when he came to get me. 'You've got to get me a job here.'

I make life decisions for the dumbest of reasons, I really do.

A week later, they hired me for the only available spot. I was given a desk, an Apple computer, the title of Junior Art Director and put in charge of creating designs for a bunch of brands. For the first few months, I sincerely and earnestly enjoyed my job. Mostly I was just grateful to have one.

J. Walter Thompson was the first and only international advertising agency in Pakistan at the time, which meant that when people asked my parents what I did, they could say proudly, 'Our son works in a multinational company.' What it meant in practical terms was that the human resources department could justify arbitrary directives by claiming it came from some nebulous head office in New York or Singapore. Beyond that, we felt little to no connection to our foreign counterparts. A year after I joined, faced with a rapidly modernising marketplace, the entire company rebranded itself as 'JWT'. Apparently initials make you cooler.

The company liked my work and, after a few months, raised my salary and gave me a promotion. This meant I had money to spend in a city that was starting to offer opportunities to spend it. Banks had only recently started offering car loans and, even though the interest rates were eye-gougingly high, everyone took advantage. The once-empty streets of Karachi instantly became gridlocked. I bought a brand-new Daihatsu Cuore, a hatchback so small it was sneered at by passing rickshaws. Every day I would park it behind the office then take the elevator up, feeling utterly futuristic as a machine scanned my palm and then a glass door unlocked with a pneumatic hiss. My desk was situated in the creative department, just along the corridor from client services and strategic planning.

Jobs would begin in client services, where clients (usually some assistant brand manager with a marketing degree and that just-upgraded-from-an-internship smell still fresh) gave instructions to an account director. The account director would then brief a strategic planner on the job. For example, a biscuit manufacturer is considering a new line of cream puffs and wants to know whether the unsuspecting audience is ready for such a paradigm shift: 'The client is thinking of making the cream pink and needs data on how this will appeal to housewives.'

While the strategic planner prepared to send an army of field agents among the citizenry to interrogate them on their emotional readiness for pink cream biscuits, the account director called a meeting to brief the creatives.

Client services and creatives historically have a turbulent relationship. Creatives think of client services as full of people too incompetent to become brand managers, who would happily fellate a company mascot if it meant keeping the client happy. Client services sees creatives as a bunch of failed artists who never had the gumption to follow their dreams and instead inflict their tortured artistry on corporate logos. Both are entirely correct in their assessment of each other.

A copywriter, an art director and the account director then sat in a side room on pastel-coloured beanbags (ad agencies love sticking random bits of childish furniture among the more traditional cubicles and swivel chairs, just to show how wildly creative they can be) and began fighting.

'The client wants the packaging to be pink,' the account director would say.

'But pink is a kiddie colour. If they want to appeal to the housewife, at least let me make it puce, which is known for its appeal to more mature audiences,' the art director argues. 'Also, the competition is pink.'

'And what about the name options I sent them?' the copywriter chimes in. 'I sent thirteen hundred names in the last two days.'

'They liked Puff Puff, Domesticatessen and Creamlicious, but want more options.'

'Look, I made a mascot,' the art director interrupts. 'Share this with them, and tell them if they don't like it they can get fucked.'

'I already shared it and they hate it. The client said it looks like a blob of pink shit with eyes. They want something new.'

'But I can't do it without feedback. What are they looking for?'

'Yeah,' the copywriter agrees. 'I need more feedback too. I don't know what they want.'

'They expect you to be more creative,' says client services.

'Fuck them!' screams the art director. 'I'm fucking creative. I won an illustration award in tenth grade. I studied graphic design for four years at university. What the fuck does the fucking client know about creativity?'

'How about Pinkalicious?' asks the copywriter.

'Look, just please give me something else. I need at least fifty names and three new mascot designs, plus options for the packaging.'

'What's the deadline?' ask the copywriter and art director in unison.

'Three o'clock today.'

'That's in half an hour!' they both scream.

'Look, I emailed you about this two days ago. Just do it.'

'Don't tell me how to do my job!' the copywriter yells. 'He's telling me how to do my job!'

'How dare you tell her how to do her job,' the art director spits, seeing this as an opportunity to score points with the copywriter, whom he has been secretly and nervously longing after for several months.

'I'm not telling you how to do your job!' says client services, who is now frustrated that he has offended the attractive copywriter, whom he has been openly ogling every time she passes his desk. 'Just please do it!'

And so on.

I would then go back to my desk and begin working on the packaging designs as well as the mascot options. The account director would announce that the deadline had been magnanimously extended till nine the next morning, which meant this would be the fourth day in a row when no one got home before midnight.

Six months of working weekends and late nights later, after several hundred packaging design options have been rejected, the client's wife decides the biscuit should be named Pinki and the mascot, a dollop of pink poo with arms and googly eyes, was to be called Pinkoo. Then the entire project is lost to a competing ad agency because they were cheaper.

I did this for three years, but the novelty wore off in the first six weeks. Along the way I got married; I got promoted twice; and I switched to another ad agency, which offered me significantly more money, but failed to mention that it only paid salaries on a whimsical basis every few months.

I also entered a deep existential crisis over the contribution I was making to the world. The only reason I was in advertising, other than the palm-scanning thingy, was because I didn't know what else to do. I knew I wanted to become a writer one day, but I had tried that and failed terribly. Depressed, I would mope around the house (to my wife's growing irritation), and I started becoming less and less tolerant of the demands that advertising made on my time.

'So what if the packaging for the tea bags is a day late?' I found myself saying. 'No one will die because of it. This job doesn't matter.' It's not the kind of attitude that endears you to colleagues who, unlike you, might actually enjoy their jobs and find that they adhered quite perfectly to their own personal versions of The Plan.

In an attempt to at least keep my writing muscles flexed, I began freelancing as a music journalist in my free time. Pakistan has a deeply impressive musical heritage. It's mostly unknown because, whenever Western journalists discover it, they always find it too incongruous, and impossible to reconcile with their notions of a Fundamentalist Islamic State. Any coverage given to it is framed within the 'musicians thrive against terrorism backdrop' narrative, which ignores the actual quality of the music. Something I was hoping to address and highlight with my reviews.

Plus, musicians are cool and I really wanted to hang out with them on the off-chance that their coolness is contagious.

3

The most famous singer from Pakistan to gain some measure of international recognition was the late Nusrat Fateh Ali Khan, who introduced the world to the devotional Sufi tradition of Qawalli. Only slightly smaller than a large mountain, Nusrat Fateh Ali Khan released songs with Peter Gabriel and Eddie Vedder (the latter song can be found on the soundtrack of the film *Dead Man Walking*). However, Qawalli can be intimidating for the new listener, featuring the sort of vocal acrobatics that would frighten a Mongolian throat singer. The Qawal needs a lifetime of training to master the staccato, machine-gun rhythm of musical scales; to attempt it without such training can leave your tongue fractured and jaw unhinged. But I wasn't drawn to the deeply traditional Qawalli; for me it was straight-up Pakistani rock'n'roll.

Ask anyone for the names of their favourite rock bands and you will get the standard response: Guns N' Roses, Led Zeppelin, the Beatles, the Rolling Stones. Ask any Pakistani who grew up in the 1990s and they will give you just one name: Junoon.

Junoon was fronted by Ali Azmat, a charismatic lead singer in the tradition of Robert Plant and Bono, except with a Pakistani accent. The guitarist was Salman Ahmad, who in his prime inspired an entire generation of Pakistani boys to piss off their parents by investing in electric guitars. On bass was an American expat named Brian O'Connell, who was married to one of the most famous models in Pakistan.

Junoon's first album debuted in 1991, right when Pakistan was indulging in one of its many flirtations with democracy. A decade-long dictatorship had ended a few years before with the death of President-Dictator Muhammad Zia Ul Haq, when a crate of mangoes on his plane turned out to be also a crate of explosives. After Zia's moustache, middle parting and fetishistic love of conservative Islam were atomised, Benazir Bhutto made her first return-from-exile. I was barely ten years old at the time and remember standing on the roof of my house and seeing her drive past on top of a bus, flashing the victory sign to her ecstatic supporters. It's the same scene that would play out almost two decades later, except that first time it didn't end in tragedy and violence.

There *was* tragedy, but that had more to do with the ineptness and endemic corruption exhibited during Benazir's time in power. Pakistan craved the freedoms and successes promised by democracy, and I still believe her failure to deliver them back then broke the nation's trust in an irreparable way. What followed was a decade of interrupted governments, each one abruptly shortened by mass protest and political opportunism. Benazir Bhutto gave way to Nawaz Sharif, a portly, balding industrialist who, most notoriously, tried to improve the economy by printing more money.

Then Nawaz Sharif was tossed out and Benazir returned. But she only managed to confirm that that everyone's previous disappointment with her had not been a mistake and she was again replaced by Nawaz Sharif, who managed this time around to enter Pakistan into the nuclear age.

Throughout this time, Pakistanis suffered through disappoint-ment, misery and then apathy – which meant the country was ready for rock'n'roll. Junoon didn't just sing the standard love anthems that pop bands had been dulling our senses with until then; they screamed about everything that was pissing us off. They combined raging guitar riffs with angry vocals and articulated the frustration we felt towards corruption and cruel governance. Ali Azmat ripped his shirt off on stage and Salman Ahmad did things with his guitar that would have made Jimi Hendrix proud.

Parents began writing letters to newspapers about the corrupting influence of Western music on the impressionable minds of the nation's youth. It was like the plot of *Footloose* played out on a national scale. There were public debates about how Brian's tight jeans were perverting teenagers, how Ali Azmat's long hair was confusing genders and how Salman Ahmad's guitar made demonic sounds that were sure to bring Allah's wrath down on our heads. The government banned their music videos and censored their songs. So of course we fucking loved them.

Inspired, I borrowed a guitar from a friend and discovered I had absolutely no musical ability. I tried singing, but the less said about that atonal croaking the better. Yet I loved music. As more Pakistani rock bands appeared throughout my teenage years, I bought all their albums and went to all their concerts. Even during my four years in America, I made sure my friends back home sent the latest CDs to me. Most of those bands would now be described as underground, mainly because Pakistan lacked the infrastructure necessary for a viable music industry during that period. But by the time I returned in 2002 that had changed.

Despite being a young country, Pakistan has a deeply honoured and long-held tradition of military coups. Every few decades, some general takes over the country, rules it for several years, then either hands it back or has it forcibly taken back by civilians. Then the whole cycle repeats.

As with all repeated patterns, there are observable similarities between each coup. It starts when a civilian president or prime minister, desperate to gain some measure of control over the armed forces despite never really having had any measure of control over anything at all, promotes some mid-level general to the rank of Chief of Army Staff. This is done with the hope of buying the loyalty of someone who was otherwise destined never to rise above military mediocrity. The newly appointed general then undergoes the same cognitive dissonance that *American Idol* winners experience when winning the top prize despite having less talent than the other singers in the competition – they believe they have earned this achievement through merit and that destiny now favours them. Emboldened by the sudden promotion, the general then grates under the yoke of civilian authority and stages a coup. It's happened so many times now that when a Chief of Army Staff *doesn't* stage a coup, people are a little disappointed and consider him an underachiever. The now former president/prime minister is shocked, dismayed and then either exiled or executed. This template was established by Pakistan's first president, Iskander Mirza (exiled), who in 1958 was overthrown by General Ayub Khan – a military dictator with a dodgy moustache and questionable hairstyle. The ninth prime minister, Zulfikar Ali Bhutto (executed), followed the format exactly and was deposed in 1977 by General Zia Ul Haq – also the owner of a dodgy moustache and questionable hairstyle. And the cycle was repeated most recently by Nawaz Sharif (exiled) in 1999, during his second go at being prime minister.

Deciding he needed a general he could control, Sharif promoted General Pervez Musharraf, over several senior and more qualified candidates, to Chief of Army Staff. (This despite Musharraf's suspiciously familiar moustache and unfortunate approach to hair styling, which should have been ample warning.) Sure enough, a year later, Sharif had to purchase a one-way ticket to Saudi Arabia and Musharraf gained entry into the exclusive club of gentlemen who can claim the title 'President-General-Dictator', where cigars are plentiful and moustache wax is available on tap.

Since the coup, Musharraf had actively encouraged the emergence of private TV channels. It was the sort of policy not normally associated with dictators, but for a time he did behave quite benevolently. Until then, the choices had been limited to two state-run channels, both heavily censored and entirely boring. Most of the private channels that first appeared were focused on news, but then someone decided it was time to create Pakistan's first twenty-four-hour music channel.

The emergence of this local version of MTV coincided with the democratisation of film-making. Any band with a computer and a video camera could now create an album and a music video and send it out into the public sphere. Bands began to form all across the country. The industry became large enough to divide itself into genres and there was enough money for them to begin indulging in stylistic experimentation. After my return from the US, I devoured this musical output hungrily. I knew I could never be a musician, but I was enamoured by their talent and charisma and wanted to be closer – hence my move into music journalism.

I sent a sample review to a local news magazine. The *Herald* was a monthly publication that allocated a few pages at the back to arts and culture reviews. The editor at the time was sufficiently impressed by my enthusiasm, if not my writing ability, to put me on his staff.

To say it paid a pittance would be to inflate the value of pittances, but I already had the advertising day job for the money. This was pure passion. All of a sudden I had access to concert passes, early review albums and one-on-one interviews. I even got to be on the judging panel of Pakistan's most prestigious music award.

Increasingly, I began to notice that the time I spent in the offices of the *Herald* were more exciting to me than the time I spent at my day job. The *Herald* was published by the privately owned Dawn Group, the same company that published Pakistan's first and thus oldest English-language daily newspaper, along with a bouquet of magazines. Headquartered in a multi-storeyed building filled with cigarette smoke and scarred wood, the offices looked and felt exactly how I imagined newspaper offices would. Every time I walked inside, I half expected Perry White to explode out of one of the interior offices, yelling, 'Great Caesar's ghost!' as he waved a copy of the *Daily Planet* over his head, Lois Lane and Clark Kent standing to attention.

Dawn, the English-language daily newspaper, had a near-infallible reputation. It had always prided itself on providing coverage and analysis that was so devoid of bias it might as well have been composed by the word-processing software itself. That it held on to this reputation while the TV channels in the country were destroying people's respect for journalism was all the more impressive.

The first forays into free-enterprise media were tentative, with GEO News testing the waters by edging away from the official narratives we were accustomed to being fed by the state-sponsored channels. It used to be that if a political party declared a city-wide shutdown in opposition to the government, we were shown file footage of shops open for business and roads choked with traffic, even though all we had to do was look out the window to see the desolation. GEO showed that shops were indeed closed and the roads really were empty.

Then, once it had established its credibility with increasingly independent news bulletins, GEO took that same credibility and pushed its head down into a bathtub full of faeces until it drowned – it started the first of many news-analysis talk shows. It was like aspiring to be the BBC and instead ending up as Fox News. Pundits hurled glasses of water at each other while politicians cursed and spat, all in front of hosts who could deliver Shakespearean monologues in a single breath. The viewing audience, who until then had only seen such theatrical debasement in tightly scripted dramas, was enraptured by the gritty realism that ratings hunger can create. More channels joined the fray, each promising more sensationalist analysis and even truthier news.

The absence of a code of ethics made the battle for ratings supremacy a bloody one. It became common for news reports to show close-up shots of bomb-blast victims, for footage of dismembered body parts to be beamed right into everyone's living rooms. Family members who had lost loved ones in tragedies had cameras pushed into their faces, with several hundred reporters yelling 'How do you feel?' even before the victim had drawn his or her final breath.

Viewers first recoiled in horror and then became utterly transfixed, managing a judgmental 'tsk tsk' as they switched from channel to channel in search of more detailed and up-to-date gore. Every week a new news channel would appear, as the snowy blizzard of empty airwaves was pushed further and further up the dial.

Newspapers, faced with redundancy, also upped the ante. Font sizes on the headlines increased, exclamation marks ran amok in columns, and the news was no longer reported and instead was predicted. Yet, somehow, *Dawn* persevered. It remained an artefact from an earlier, more discerning time – black and white pages of neatly spaced type, conveying information in a flatly emotionless voice, which somehow made the increasingly bad news more palatable. And the news was getting really bad.

By 2006 the facade of calm progress so successfully created by General Musharraf had begun to wear thin and suicide bombings became a regular occurrence.

Analysts still get into violent punch-ups over why things started deteriorating. Academic papers, documentaries and even bestselling paperbacks have all put forward theories of varying credibility. Did things look good for a while because Musharraf was keeping the real problems out of the public eye by constraining them to the Pak–Afghan border, where cameramen rarely go and life has always been too brutal and harsh for the rest of the civilised world to worry about? Or was it because, in the end, no matter how much you try, terrorism is like the dinosaurs in *Jurassic Park*, irrepressibly finding a way to live. One thing everyone could agree on was that it all went back to those crucial moments after the planes smashed into the twin towers of New York's World Trade Center. As soon as it was clear that America needed to deal with the Taliban and Al-Qaeda in Afghanistan, it fixed its Sauron glare on Pakistan for support. In later interviews, Musharraf claimed that the message sent by President Bush was for Pakistan to support the US in the coming war against terrorism or he would bomb Pakistan 'back to the stone age'.

And so began the War on Terror. Militant extremists were pushed out of Afghanistan by American forces, and retreated across the border into Pakistan. (It's worth noting that describing it as a 'border' makes it sound a great deal more tangible than it really is. Think of it less like a defensible barricade and more like a vague point of view.) Those terrorists then found refuge in Pakistan's cities, which are too large and overpopulated for effective policing.

At this point, an analyst with a degree in South Asian politics, not to mention a research post in a Washington DC think-tank, will jump up and yell that there is enough evidence to prove Pakistan's intelligence agencies helped camouflage the terrorists so that said agencies could then use them for their own strategic goals. In response, a retired Pakistani general who has dinner monthly with US State Department officials in Islamabad, not to mention his contribution of weekly columns for local newspapers, will scream that America helped create a lot of those terrorist groups in the 1980s to fight Soviet Communism and tasked Pakistan with maintaining them. And besides, more Pakistani soldiers and civilians have been killed by those terrorists than have Americans, so continued support for them is just not true.

The two will start hurling abuse at each other on Twitter, write arguments in international newspapers and get paid handsomely for media appearances. Meanwhile, the bombs will continue to go off, bullets will be fired and people will continue to die.

4

Violence entered my life barely three weeks after I returned to Karachi. Before joining J. Walter Thompson, I interned at a small start-up web design firm – twelve people crammed into an office overlooking a smog-choked road near Karachi's industrial district. A few days into my internship, the receptionist answered the phone, then began screaming hysterically.

The accountant had gone down to the bank to withdraw cash for everyone's salaries. Someone inside the bank saw him carrying over a hundred thousand rupees in a brown envelope, intercepted him right outside the bank and took it from him. When he protested, he was shot twice in the stomach.

A crowd gathered around to gawp at the skinny little man bleeding out on the pavement. He pleaded for help and, when none was offered, called the office with his own mobile phone.

At the time, almost everyone I worked with had left for lunch. I was trying to finish off a project and so was eating a plate of biryani at my desk when my meal was interrupted by the receptionist's shrill scream. She explained what had happened, and a web designer and I rushed down to my small Cuore parked outside. The bank was half a mile away; I swerved through traffic, horn blaring. When we got there, the accountant was still lying on the ground, blood pumping

36

in thinning rivulets from behind his fingers, over a hundred people watching mutely. With some effort, the web designer and I carried him to the back seat of the car. He was, amazingly, still awake and lucid, although unable to talk from the pain and shock.

Horn blaring once again, I drove us to a private hospital nearby. There, attendants carried him inside as a doctor rushed up to us.

'What happened?' he asked, a middle-aged man in a white coat.

'He was robbed,' I said, still inside the car. The back seat looked like the inside of an abattoir. 'The thief shot him.'

The doctor signalled for us to stay in the car as he disappeared inside the emergency ward. Five minutes later, the accountant was wheeled back out, strapped to a gurney. His white shirt was now a deep maroon and he still had his hands over the open stomach wound that hadn't stopped bleeding.

'We aren't allowed to process gunshot victims here,' said the doctor as we stared at him aghast. 'You have to take him to Jinnah Hospital, where the police will file the First Action Report.'

'But he'll die,' we screamed.

'Nothing can be done, sorry. Those are the rules.'

I've never been able to inflict violence convincingly. Growing up, I was a skinny boy who managed to avoid being bullied because of a razor-sharp tongue. Bigger boys fear mocking nicknames more than a defensive punch and they left me alone. In my teens I took martial arts classes for several years and learned to be quite deadly, as long as there was a referee around to deduct points for hitting the face or below the belt. Other than one fight, when I was twelve, over an arcade game loss – it ended with me vaulting over a house wall while five boys gave chase – I had managed to avoid situations where a flared temper might lead to violence, mostly because I was scared of getting the shit kicked out of me.

Had the doctor known this, he might have been less frightened when I opened the boot of the car, pulled out the car jack and threatened to bash him over the head if he didn't help the accountant. Lacking knowledge of my personal history, and thus being intimidated by a skinny boy with thick spectacles swinging a metal rod in the vicinity of his head, he assented.

By the time an ambulance arrived from Jinnah Hospital, the accountant's wounds had been bandaged and an IV drip connected to his arm. Amazingly, the tough bastard was still awake. The web designer and I followed the ambulance to the large public hospital several miles away.

Jinnah Hospital is, even as public hospitals go, a tremendously wretched place. The doctors who work there provide medical aid with shockingly limited resources to an unrelenting flood of human misery. I had never been there before and was taken aback by what I saw, smelled and heard. Families wailed; the corridors were stained with chewed betel-nut spit; people sat in the waiting room with their limbs attached by the thinnest of muscle fibres, bleeding all over the floor; cats fattened on discarded organs brazenly roamed in and out of operating theatres.

The accountant survived. By the time he returned to work a few months later, I had moved on to the ad agency.

Sometimes I wonder why I wasn't more traumatised by what I experienced. It isn't often that you spend your weekend scrubbing blood out of the back seat of your car. Had I been sensible, I would probably have driven straight from the hospital to the airport and taken the first plane back to America, but the thought never occurred to me. Instead, I tamped down the entire experience with a simple rationalisation: I was physically fine, wasn't I? Nothing had happened to me. So no big deal, right? No drama.

Four weeks back and I was already thinking like a Karachiite again. It's the same thought process that keeps everyone else in the city from surrendering to insanity. When you are constantly facing the prospect of violent death, the only rational response is to throw your hands up in defeat and lock yourself in the bathroom to spend the rest of your life shivering in the bathtub while you wait for the suicide bombers, serial killers and murderous thieves to find their way to your door and end it all for you. But rational is not sensible. Sensible people get on with their lives. They go to their jobs, drop their children at school and shop for groceries. Death, no matter who brings it, will come unannounced and so there is no point in waiting around for it. Everyone in Karachi has things to do and places to be. The potential for unexpected interruption in that schedule cannot allow its derailment.

I was confronted with the best evidence of this attitude in May 2004, when a car packed with explosives detonated less than half a mile away from the advertising agency office. The entire building thrummed, every surface vibrating like a tuning fork as computers fell off desks and chairs tipped over. Karachi is built on a fault line and so everyone is used to the odd tremor every couple of years, but the reverberations of a bomb blast are instantly distinguishable; they resonate at a deeper register, like the difference between strumming a sitar and a bass guitar. We ran to the windows to see a column of black smoke rising in the distance, from the direction of the school where my mother taught. In a panic, I called her mobile phone.

She answered immediately, and told me she had been inside the school when the bomb went off right near the front gate. They were probably targeting the US consul general's residence across the road and not a group of English teachers.

'I'm okay,' she said.

'Still, you should go home. In fact, you should not go back to school. It's not safe there anymore.'

'Oh don't be silly,' my mother said, amused by my (to her) dramatic overreaction. 'I didn't die, did I? So everything is fine.'

The school reopened two days later, and not a single teacher or student withdrew. The consul general, meanwhile, moved to a more secure location.

--------- • ---------

A month later, after parking my car near the JWT office, I was walking to work with a horde of other employees. Security around our building had been amped up because of the proximity to the US consulate, with cargo containers narrowing access to the road in front of the office. As we all crossed from the car park, we heard a small explosion in the distance, followed by the unmistakable rattle of gunfire. At any other time of day, we might have confused it for celebratory fireworks, but at 8.45 am it could only be gunshots and explosives.

Later, we learned it was a terrorist attack on the Karachi Corps Commander's motorcade just a few hundred metres up the road. It was so close that, just as we registered the sounds of a pitched gun battle, actual bullets began spitting to the ground around us. I looked up to see the police officers who were tasked with keeping this area secure running through a door cut into the side of the container and shutting it behind them. Left on our own, we all scampered for the office, making it inside with no injuries.

Eleven people died that morning – army officers and policemen, cut down by a torrent of gunfire and grenades. All of this was close enough to the office for us to watch it unfold from the windows above. Yet no client deadlines were altered, nor did anyone ask to go home. We were physically fine, and so work continued.

I began to feel as though violence was encircling my life in the city, tightening its arc with every bomb blast. Yet being in advertising highlighted my ignorance about the world erupting around me. Every time I visited the *Dawn* offices, I would hear journalists and editors discussing the growing attacks on the country by terrorist groups. Their discussions seemed better informed and more intelligently analytical than the conspiracy-theorist pap that everyone else was swapping.

Pakistanis are addicted to conspiracy theories. Everything that happens in the country provides evidence of the existence of multiple extravagant conspiracies simultaneously. It's similar to the American fascination with Area 51, for example, but also reveals where Pakistanis believe the true power lies.

In America, the popular conspiracy theories are that the government has UFOs in a secret airbase, or that the government is putting fluoride in the water supply or implanting microchips in people's brains. American conspiracy theories all involve their government having greater control over the citizenry than is most likely true.

In Pakistan, however, the conspiracy theories are always about how the CIA is behind everything, or the Indian RAW agency, or the Mossad or the Illuminati, or just Jews and Christians in general. Pakistani conspiracy theories are always about someone else's government secretly controlling our lives. This shows how little faith Pakistanis have in their own government. For them to believe that the Pakistani government is actually organised enough to have any measure of control over anything isn't a conspiracy theory – it's a conspiracy fantasy.

Conspiracy theories are addictive because they provide the illusion of control. It is more comforting to believe that someone – anyone – is racing the car towards the edge of the cliff than to acknowledge that it's heading there of its own accord.

At *Dawn*, however, I was confronted with the more upsetting, and simultaneously enlightening, details of reality. A reporter would explain how the problem faced by the military in combating the extremist groups was that the same extremist philosophies had been bred into the rank-and-file soldiers during Zia Ul Haq's time. The dictator had wanted armed forces who would fanatically obey any of his orders and discovered those orders were more convincing when couched in the language of Jihad. 'Take that hill or die trying' is not as effective an order as 'Take that hill in the name of Allah and, if you die trying, you'll go to heaven as a martyr'. The madrasas that now created the terrorists who killed civilians were once the recruiting grounds for the military. Shifting allegiances away from Jihadist culture after 9/11 had left many soldiers feeling as though their beliefs had been betrayed. And so the military was fighting an internal as well as an external enemy. And in both cases, the enemy was just as Pakistani as they were.

Meanwhile, in my advertising agency office, the blame was being placed on the Israeli Mossad, Indian RAW agents and the Illuminati – all being funded by the CIA and MI6.

I started to view journalism as the only sensible prism through which to view what was happening to Pakistan. I imagined it was very much like putting on a pair of spectacles for the first time and having the blurs and smudges sharpen into visual information you could process and thus, if need be, avoid. I was still uneasy with the sensationalist abyss that the TV channels were spelunking and so I focused my job search on the print side, with *Dawn* being at the top of my very short list. Word must have got out about my enthusiasm because, at the end of 2005, I was invited to meet with someone from within *Dawn*.

Shakeel Masud was a tall man, with broad shoulders and a Sean-Connery-meets-Anthony-Hopkins-by-way-of-the-Khyber-Pass face. He had a neatly trimmed grey beard framing his face in strict angles; his voice was so deep that, to catch all his words, you needed to ram an iron rod into the ground and then translate the vibrations it registered using seismic analysis. Over a cup of coffee in a hotel lobby, he told me that *Dawn* was about to start a TV channel of its own – one that reflected the ethos of the newspaper and would try to insert a calm, credible voice into the hysterical media landscape.

'When it launches in a year,' he rumbled, 'how would you like to be part of the marketing team?'

My excitement at hearing about what would eventually be known as Dawn News TV was shaded by disappointment at the offer of a marketing role. I could already imagine sitting in a cubicle off to the side, ignoring a revenue-generation spreadsheet while longingly watching the news department. I also thought that, if I had to spend another year in advertising, I'd end up in one of those news stories about a disgruntled employee gunning down co-workers because he was tired of being told to make the fucking logo bigger.

'I don't want to work in marketing,' I told him. 'I want to be in news. Anything at all, I'll do it. Just let me in the newsroom, please.'

A week later, I resigned from the ad agency and walked into the *Dawn* offices with an 'employee' badge. The salary was half of what I had been earning and the channel was too nascent even to offer a job title, but I was giddy with joy.

5

Dawn News TV started with seven people, in an out-of-the-way room in the bowels of the *Dawn* newspaper building. I was employee number six. Not counted in this number were the CEO, Shakeel Masud himself, and the executive director, a young woman named Nazafreen Saigol. Her family was the money behind the channel and we always assumed she was there to make sure the money wasn't being wasted. I was keen to prove than an ex-advertising graphic designer with a degree in English wasn't wastage and so pledged myself to the channel with the kind of fanatical loyalty demanded of secret brotherhoods in Ivy League universities.

With me was Wajahat Khan, a bald alpha male with the demeanour of a silverback gorilla on the rampage, who was heading the 'international desk'. Wajahat went on to host the Dawn News equivalent of the BBC's *Hard Talk*, pinning down politicians with his growling voice and threatening finger stabs. Sahar Habib, probably the most intimidatingly intelligent person I've ever met, had escaped GEO News; Mikail Lotia used to host a business analysis show on the only all-business TV channel in the country and we instantly bonded over a shared love of geek culture; Khawer Khan was, like me, an idealistic newbie to the world of journalism, as was Mohsin Abbas, recently returned from university in Texas with a Houston accent.

Finally there was Sanaa Ahmed, an émigré from the newspaper, who had once been a lawyer and was now a chain-smoking editor. Sanaa and Wajahat were tasked with training the rest of us until more people joined, and so for the first month they took turns providing us with insights into the workings of a twenty-four-hour news channel. Unfortunately, they disagreed on almost every single point and within a week we had learned to fade out their screaming matches while we sat around fantasising about what the channel would be like.

I was first told that I would be in charge of the news ticker that runs horizontally across the bottom of every news channel. Then, a few days later, I was moved up to the international desk. None of this meant anything as the only equipment we had up till then were our own personal laptops and a few chairs and desks. Every day, Sahar, Mikail, Mohsin, Khawar and I would sit around carefully studying BBC news bulletins and discussing theories about the role of journalism in society, while Wajahat and Sanaa would outline assignments for us.

One day we were all told to go out and come back within three hours with an interview each. That we had no cameras with which to film those interviews meant we would have to transcribe them. So we all went for lunch instead, and conducted mock interviews with one another over burgers and fries.

Mikail left us for a few weeks to appear as an ISI agent in Angelina Jolie's Daniel Pearl biopic. He would call us periodically to tell us about how he got to play with Maddox and what a treat it was to work with 'Angie'. Naturally, we hated him immensely.

In my second week, I got into a screaming match with Sanaa and to this day controversy exists over who won by shouting louder. She says she did and everyone else in the triple-storey office says I did. The print journalists, all studied seriousness and pipe-smoking, tutted loudly every time we crossed their paths and in our heads we created an instant mythology of the young clashing with the old.

In the first few weeks, our ranks swelled in dribs and drabs. We were joined by Osama Bin Javaid, a BBC reporter who was destined to be finger-banged in every international airport because of his name; Ali Mustafa, who spoke with the dramatic theatricality of a Shakespearean actor, ending every sentence with a knowing wink and a rehearsed smile; and Khanzada Sahib, a crime reporter from the print world who had spent the nineties sifting through gunny sacks filled with body parts so he might identify the victim for both the police and his newspaper. Khanzada Sahib was my idea of a journalist: a cigarette perpetually between his fingers, a green flak jacket with enough pockets to make Batman's utility belt envious and the name of every beat cop in the city scrawled inside his skull.

When we weren't out pretending to complete vague assignments, we would sit around the cavernous office we had all been sentenced to and listen to Khanzada's stories. We each had visions of what we wanted the channel to be like and the one point of agreement for all of us was that it be nothing like the other news channels. Our ideal was the BBC, while everyone else was trying to be CNN.

Five weeks in, a surge of new employees reminded us that the channel was actually going to be more than just a handful of us with laptops and nebulous dreams. We walked in to work one morning to discover over thirty people spilling out of our office. Aspiring and experienced journalists from the other major cities of Pakistan, all brought together by the same reverence for the Dawn name and curiosity about how that would translate into television. Most of them were the same age as me – twenty-somethings who had decided they didn't want to work in banks or become lawyers and were tempted by the adrenaline-soaked siren song of journalism. The rest, already working in media, had been enticed by the transition to television. We all mingled and introduced ourselves and then, once we were acquainted, Shakeel Masud introduced us to our trainers.

Setting up a TV channel requires more than just a staff and equipment. Even if all the machines are plugged in, the camera batteries charged and anchor earpieces cleaned, without training it is impossible to actually do anything. And we weren't just joining an already-established channel; we were mostly first-timers building a channel from the ground up.

That everyone else was as much of a novice as I was made it a great deal easier for me to admit to my own ignorance, which is not something that comes easily to me. When in doubt, I always subscribe to the fake-it-till-you-make-it approach. When I joined advertising, even though I knew almost nothing about what the job entailed, I camouflaged that inexperience with a blustering mix of confidence and arrogance. If you say things with enough volume and emphasis, I discovered, people think you know what you're talking about. Of course it's only a short-term strategy, because after a while people will stop finding you boldly confident and just start thinking of you as 'that obnoxious guy who yells all the time'. But it buys you just enough time to learn the basics fast and then extrapolate the rest.

This was a skill I had learned in college. Perpetually broke, I was delighted to discover that course books would be refunded up to a week after purchase. So at the start of every term, I would buy all the books, spend an entire week using every waking moment to consume as much of them as possible, and then return them to the shop for a refund. That way, I had enough knowledge of the texts to make an impression on the teachers in the first few weeks, making sure I answered all posited questions and engaged loudly in any class discussions, while having enough cash to buy comics instead.

By the time the details of the texts had faded from my memory – usually halfway through the semester – I had impressed the teacher sufficiently to let my participation slacken. At the advertising job, I couldn't cram during the first few days of my employment, but I could let everyone else think I knew what I was talking about while scrambling to discover exactly what I *should* be talking about. But at the channel, not knowing what to do didn't make me uniquely illiterate – it put me at the base level required of all of us for training to start.

The trainers who came in to instruct us were the same people who had trained the first of the GEO staff some years before. They had also helped launch news channels in Greece, India and South Africa; their experience with television news was as old as the medium. Leading the group was Ken Tiven, a short American who had the beard and jovial friendliness of Santa Claus. That is, if Santa cursed a lot. Like, a whole lot. It was Ken who oversaw the rest of the trainers and brought them in and out of the country, depending on when their skill sets were needed. He had been there during the first days of CNN, but at Dawn he found himself working under budgetary constraints that would enable him to execute a new concept for modern journalism that he was concocting. The idea was that the channel's payroll wouldn't be bloated with cameramen and reporters and video editors; instead, everyone would be their own cameraman, reporter and video editor. You would go out into the field with a tripod and camera, and record the footage needed; then you would flip the LCD display on the side of the camera around so you could stand in front of it and see yourself framed in the shot as you delivered your report. After that you'd take it all back to the office and edit it using the basic video-editing software that comes bundled with

Apple laptops. The channel would pay one person to do the job of three and we would all get the added bonus of multiple skill sets.

These days, of course, every reporter working for every newspaper, TV channel and website can do those things – along with most teenagers, housewives and even my grandfather. At the time, though, everyone reacted as if he was asking them to create a photorealistic painting while doing one-armed push-ups. Being one of the only people with actual experience with an Apple computer (probably the only useful skill gained from my time in advertising), I found myself bumped to the head of the class.

Helping Ken was Bob Yuna, also an American, who coordinated the different instructors and assessed which areas of specialisation any of us would need, while finding time to discuss classic films and old jazz standards with Wikipedia-esque depth. There was a cameraman from South Africa, who taught us not only how to focus and white balance the camera properly, but also how to use the tripod for self-defence; a copy editor from Bangladesh, who taught us how to write entire stories in three-minute, one-minute and fourteen-second slices; and a video editor from Germany, who provided us with professional Hollywood-editing-suite-capable skills in a couple of days.

My favourite instructor, though, was Walter Rodgers. Walter was the former CNN Jerusalem bureau chief, who had worked as Moscow bureau chief for ABC (America) News during the height of the Cold War and was one of the first Western journalists into Afghanistan after Kabul fell to the Americans. He had a voice like granite cracking and could deliver a broadcast-ready monologue covering any topic inside of a few seconds. Walter was the guy other journalists wanted to grow up to become. He wasn't as famous as most of the talking heads on American news media, and had thus retained all his credibility.

All the trainers were provided with constant armed guards and they were made to adhere to a tight curfew, for their own safety. This drove Walter into a perpetual grumble and, when he wasn't teaching us how to speak to a camera and organise our thoughts while being in hypothetically frightening situations, he was trying to find a way to slip past his minders and explore Karachi.

By the end of 2006, there were enough of us that we had to be split into two groups – morning and evening shifts, with a fortnightly rotation allowing us some semblance of a social life. It was our first taste of the experience that leaves most journalists complete social pariahs. Finding time to meet other people becomes enough of a challenge; actually talking to those people is even more difficult. Civilians are ill-informed about the world they live in and think filling in their weekly timesheets and Excel spreadsheets is work pressure. Journalists fancy themselves as being at the frontline of human experience – divers into the deepest seas of reality, plunging to extreme pressures that would crush a submarine and turn a chartered accountant or marketer into jelly. The only other life forms capable of surviving at those depths are doctors and soldiers.

Slowly our equipment was upgraded. It started with a storage room that had been soundproofed with mattresses; a table was dragged into its centre, and behind it anchors-in-training stood and delivered mock news to a single handheld camera. That footage was then edited and reviewed. The instructors took us through all the different roles of a newsroom and then began choosing everyone's specialisation, based on interests and natural abilities. Ali Mustafa was, of course, the first one to move on to being a news anchor, having exactly the right mix of screen presence and overstated gravitas. Others became reporters and desk editors.

It was decided that Mikail, Sahar and I had the right temperament to become panel producers. We would need to take the news stories and footage compiled by the others, then direct the anchor's presentation of them and try to compress it all into a coherent news bulletin. It meant being the brunt of several egos and opinions and trying to distil it all, while staying true to the stated goals of the channel. Seeing as how I had been brought in to write the news ticker and then moved up to scouring the internet for international news stories, this was a great deal more than I had imagined myself capable of, or ever being entrusted with.

Every moment not in the Dawn offices, we would obsess over the way other channels ran their news. I watched every bulletin on Al Jazeera English and BBC News, fixating on camera angles and anchor switches. Even today, I get an electric thrill from watching how breaking news stories unfold in live news environments.

By March 2007 we had relocated to what is still the headquarters of Dawn News: a custom-built office near Karachi's West Wharf district, shaded by an oil refinery and with a view – if you can see over the high walls – of the shipping port. Inside were two large glass studios, one for the news and the other for current affairs programs, fitted with remote-controlled cameras and teleprompter screens. Attached to the studio, behind soundproofed doors, was the control room, comprising a bank of monitors blazing with footage, sound-mixing boards and the panel producer's console.

When standing at that console I could scroll or edit the script being fed to the anchor, move each camera inside the studio with a video-game joystick, switch between the cameras and any incoming footage using a flat panel studded with multicoloured buttons called a video mixer, activate on-screen graphics and talk directly into the anchor's ear through my headset microphone. It was all I could do not to sport a visible erection.

The channel wasn't due to launch officially for a few more weeks, but we had already begun sending out a test transmission that could be watched by select people in the government and by the major cable operators. Even without official viewers, we had begun operating as a twenty-four-hour channel in every way. Sahar, Mikail and I rotated through daily eight-hour shifts as panel producers; a roster of anchors delivered the news under the strict scrutiny of an instructor on loan from Al Jazeera's Kuala Lumpur bureau; and reporters were already out in the city chasing after exclusives and harassing people for sound bites. That we had no actual viewing audience, beyond a few censors, meant some of the teething problems could be identified and sorted before the channel went live.

So, for example, the next time a fly sat on the news anchor's eye and refused to move while she struggled to read from her teleprompter, while I stood uselessly behind the door inside my control room trying to use any latent telekinetic ability I might have to brush it away, I could instead simply cut to stock footage of something vaguely related to the story and buy her time to punch herself in the face and then run for cover as I blasted the winged son-of-a-bitch with two cans of insecticide. Hypothetically speaking.

--------- • ---------

On 9 March 2007, an increasingly unpopular President Musharraf overestimated his powers and underestimated his opponents by suspending the Chief Justice of Pakistan. He might have assumed this would be a non-issue, seeing as how the same Chief Justice had earlier been part of the Supreme Court that legalised the president's dictatorship, but it was a fatal miscalculation.

Iftikhar Chaudhry, the Chief Justice, who sported a questionable moustache and a distractingly active lazy eye, had been angling for a confrontation with Musharraf for several months prior to this, focusing his attention on several missing-persons cases brought to the courts. As part of Pakistan's complicity in the War on Terror, many people had disappeared without a trace, most – it was suspected – handed over to the CIA for torture and interrogation. That their families were not told of their whereabouts, or even if they were still alive, was quite obviously creating unrest, and increasingly it began to seem as though Musharraf was selling out his own countrymen in exchange for American support. At least that was the narrative being constructed by the courts and in the media.

Deciding to deal with this in the decisive manner that had made him so popular with American interviewers, Musharraf summoned the Chief Justice to a private meeting, and then told him he was fired. But Chaudhry refused to accept Musharraf's authority over him and attempted to return to the courts. Along the way he was mistreated by the police and then placed under house arrest. Lawyers around the nation rioted. Within hours every cameraman in every city was sending us footage of men and women in black suits being beaten by the police as they screamed in protest.

'It's like the end of *Matrix Reloaded*,' one of the other producers said, watching several hundred lawyers barrelling towards a frightened police officer, then getting beaten back with water cannons and batons.

I'll admit to underestimating the significance of what had just happened. I asked Azhar Abbas what he thought of all this, as the lawyers began demanding the Chief Justice's reinstatement with increasing vigour, and he said, 'This is going to be a lot larger than you realise.'

'I wish we were already broadcasting to everyone,' I said. 'What a missed opportunity to cover some breaking news.'

'This is Pakistan,' Azhar said with a grim smile. 'There's going to be much more opportunity to cover breaking news.'

He was right. By May, Iftikhar Chaudhry's house arrest had been lifted and he was touring the country, stopping in the major cities to deliver impassioned speeches about the supremacy of law over the corrupting powers of a dictatorship. At every stop he was carried aloft by masses of lawyers, cheering him with the sort of hysterical frenzy usually reserved for teenage girls at a One Direction concert. His rally in Lahore having been deemed a success, he set his eye on Karachi. Which is when things turned ugly.

Legal battles are still being fought over who tried to stop Iftikhar Chaudhry's arrival in Karachi. Witnesses disappear and lawyers turn up dead, so those court cases are unlikely to ever return a verdict. Therefore, officially there is no single person or group of people who carries the blame. But Karachiites know who it was; it's just that we're not stupid enough to say it aloud. In a city where you can die at any time and in many ways, why give death a reason to come after you?

Back then, as now, large parts of the city were controlled by a single criminal organisation, masquerading as a political party with ethnic roots. In the years since Musharraf, that organisation has seen its power recede, with other political parties hungrily taking bloody mouthfuls of whatever is left behind. But in 2007, Musharraf knew who to call.

If I'm being vague, it's because you can take the boy out of Karachi, but you can't take Karachi's fears out of the boy.

That day I had the 8 am to 4 pm shift, so I left my home much earlier than Chaudhry's expected noon arrival. It was fortunate that I did, as all the major roads were barricaded. The drive to work normally took me half an hour and cut right through the centre of Karachi on a continuous wide road. However, it had been blocked off with shipping containers, each wallpapered with the flags of the political party that had been tasked with keeping Iftikhar Chaudhry out of the city.

When I called my office to tell them I'd be taking a longer, more circuitous route around the city, they asked me to provide an update on the roads for the bulletin, but to avoid any mention of the political party responsible for the blockades.

'We don't want them to come after you,' the desk editor told me, only half joking.

I reached work an hour after my shift had officially started. The panel producer I was relieving wished me luck as he handed over the headset and then began his own trek home. Every reporter and cameraman we had in the city was already deployed; even anchors not assigned to the studio had been sent out. Then the whole city waited for Iftikhar Chaudhry's plane to land, like a punch.

--------- • ---------

By late evening, when it became clear that he could not leave the airport without being killed, the Chief Justice took a plane back to Islamabad. Over eight hundred of his supporters had been arrested, just for daring to cheer his arrival; almost fifty people had been killed and over a hundred injured. I heard of reporters having their cars hijacked by gunmen, and others taking cover under parked vans as gunfights played out in front of them. One TV channel was unfortunate enough to have a major firefight conducted in its car park, with journalists broadcasting footage of their own cars being set alight by political-party thugs.

A great deal of the fighting, it turned out, was across the road from my house, where my mother and wife peeked from the roof at the carnage unfolding close by. At one point I called my wife to ask how close they were to the violence and she stuck her phone out the window so I could hear the rattle of gunfire.

A couple of hours after my shift should have ended, the producer tasked with relieving me managed to get to the office. He lived close by. I called a reporter stationed at the airport to ask whether it was safe to head for home.

'I can still see a lot of smoke across the city,' he told me, 'but none of it is from new fires. So I guess you can risk it.'

For the first ten minutes of the drive, I found myself noting how pleasant it was to travel through the city when the streets were so empty. The moment I had that thought, I realised – like a character in a badly written suspense movie – that the city was indeed *too* empty. Mine was the only car on the road.

Coming around the first major bend, I saw a gigantic boulder lying in the middle of the road and had to swerve around it. I'm still not sure where they found a boulder and who it was being used to crush. A few feet ahead lay a dead body, which I also swerved around. Then another. At the third dead body – a man lying face down in a puddle of crushed glass, each shard glinting pink – I began to seriously question my decision to drive home. Which was when I saw the mob. Directly ahead were over a hundred men, all armed, blocking the middle of the road.

I swung into a police station to my left, where I found several police officers sitting around a table, sipping tea as they watched the mob in the distance.

'Who are they?' I asked.

'Allah knows,' replied one officer, slurping his tea.

'Why don't you go and ask them?' suggested another, eyeing my press badge.

'I need to get home. Do you think they'll let me?'

'You'll never know until you ask,' observed the first officer.

'Don't forget to say "please",' said the second.

Having come this far, I decided to try. Maybe it was because I knew home was just five minutes beyond them, and driving all the way back to the office meant seeing the dead bodies again. I got back in my car and drove slowly up to the crowd. As I approached, I held up my press badge, waving it slowly to make sure they saw it.

Pretty soon the car could go no further, not without actually driving over the men armed with machine guns, which is one of those things you try to avoid.

One of them took my press badge from me, studied it for a few seconds, then asked where I was going.

'Home,' I said. 'I've finished work.'

'You work for *Dawn* newspaper?' he asked.

'Yes,' I replied, deciding this was not the time and place to explain that I was actually employed by a TV channel connected to the newspaper.

He turned to the others and gestured for them to let me pass. 'He works for *Dawn*,' he said, then tossed my badge back into the car.

The crowd parted. I thanked the man, and then sped the rest of the way home, my tyres crunching noisily over the broken glass.

6

The shift rotations meant that on 25 May, the day that Dawn News officially launched its Open Test Transmission (this was different from the previous test transmission phase in that anyone with a cable connection could watch the channel, as opposed to it being limited to government officials as before), I was again the producer working the panel. The launch was made all the more auspicious by the fact that President Musharraf had decided to inaugurate the channel. In preparation for his arrival, the road leading to the office was freshly tarred and so, for a few weeks at least, no longer resembled the cratered surface of the moon. Military security took over the entire building, with guards checking and then rechecking all our identification every time we went to use the toilet. Even though we had being functioning like an active news channel for several months at that point, nerves were frayed and Azhar Abbas had to remind each one of us that he had faith in our abilities.

His reassurance served to keep nausea at bay and by evening, when the president arrived with his extensive entourage, I felt confident I wasn't going to press the wrong switches and activate some heretofore unknown self-destruct sequence. The plan was for Musharraf to deliver a speech in the exterior compound that would be broadcast live; I would then switch over to the freshly polished studio, where our anchors would read an overwritten description of the goals and ambitions of the channel. If all went smoothly, anyone in the country could henceforth watch Dawn News, albeit with a tiny 'test transmission' graphic present in the corner of the screen, to manage expectations.

The entire staff was present, everyone I had spent the last year training with, all of us more emotionally invested in this than almost anything we had ever done before in our lives. The anchors presenting the inaugural bulletin were Ali Mustafa and Naveen Naqvi. Naveen was a familiar face to Pakistanis who had lived through the 1990s; she had started out as a model and then gone on to host the country's first music show before working for an American news channel during the run-up to the Afghan war. Her crisp delivery balanced Ali's more bombastic approach to news reading, and enough people in the office had a crush on her for my own infatuation to be excused.

Musharraf came with his own OB van, run by the state television channel. During his lengthy speech about the importance of a free and fair media as a symbol of democratic growth, all I was required to do was cut to the feed from the van outside. Then, once the speech was done, I took over. Slowly panning down a camera stapled to the ceiling of the studio, I gave the anchors their cue to begin. Their reading was flawless and every camera switch we had rehearsed went off without an error. The first launch bulletin of Dawn News, as seen by the general public, was a success.

The moment the anchors completed their introduction and threw to a pre-recorded mini-documentary about the history of the newspaper *Dawn*, the newsroom erupted into cheers and applause. Azhar Abbas clapped me on the back and told me I had done well. I turned to thank and congratulate him in turn. And then the lights went out.

Electricity in Karachi can charitably be described as inconsistent. Unannounced power outages are frequent and everyone who can afford it owns a generator. Those who can't own candles and matchbooks. Dawn News – like all other TV channels, offices and factories – runs entirely on privately generated electricity. And if, on that day, we had stayed on our generator, things would have been fine. However, the generator was placed close to where Musharraf was to deliver his speech and its rumbling would have drowned out his voice. Therefore, the generator was switched off and assurances given by the Karachi Electric Supply Corporation that electricity would run uninterrupted through the evening. Apparently it was too much to ask for.

In an instant, the entire building was plunged into darkness and the broadcast was switched off. As Musharraf's security threw him over their shoulders and dived into their cars, one of our electricians tried to activate our generator at the same time that the KESC switched everything back on. There was a small explosion and the electrician was thrown several feet backwards, landing in a shuddering mess on the ground, black smoke belching from his mouth.

By the time we got power back on half an hour later, the electrician was in a hospital ward (thanks to the newly paved roads, he got there just in time to survive the near-fatal dose of electricity), Musharraf was speeding back towards the airport and the rest of us were wondering whether this was some sort of omen. As a precaution, to ward off bad luck, Shakeel Masud and Azhar Abbas had a black goat sacrificed in the compound where Musharraf had just been standing. You can never be too careful.

--------- • ---------

Over the next few months, the nation fell deeper into chaos and I watched it all from my control panel. The only field experience I got in those first few months was when, thanks to a shortage of reporters, I was asked to take a camera out and grab a few minutes of footage at a lawyers' rally. Agitation against Musharraf's dictatorship was growing and at the forefront of every protest was the legal fraternity. Men and women in black suits articulated the increasing discontent with fanciful chants and fist-pumping.

The protest march I filmed was taking place just outside the city's High Court and I expected I would walk up, put my camera on the tripod, film a few minutes of people slinging slogans and then head back to the office. However, the lawyers had decided that their oppression wasn't just at the hands of Musharraf and his government allies but also the media. It was a strange decision, given that the success of their movement could be attributed to the blanket coverage granted to it by the news channels. Regardless, instead of debating the finer points of how much time their story was being given on air in comparison to other pressing issues of the day, they began to beat us instead. A reporter and cameraman from another channel were the first to be swallowed by the horde of suits.

I watched in horror as a dozen black coats descended like Azkaban's Dementors, shoving the pair to the ground and then proceeding to kick the shit out of them. I was still filming the assault when they turned to see me standing behind them, angling for a better view. By the time the first lawyer grabbed me, I had already pulled the camera off the tripod. I used it to bludgeon his hand away from my shirt, then turned to see several more bearing down on me.

Deciding sarcastic commentary would not provide me enough protection, I remembered the training we had received from the South African cameraman. Wielding the bulky tripod like a fencing foil, I managed to connect its metal legs with enough faces to convince them to fall back. Then, taking advantage of the brief moment of shock they were suffering, I turned and ran. By the time they decided to give chase, I was already in my car and speeding away.

--------- • ---------

When, in the first week of July, a mosque in Islamabad was besieged by the army after militants inside refused to surrender, I was grateful to view the entire proceedings from the safety of my control room. Not that the panel producers were immune from stress. What became known as the Lal Masjid Siege went on for almost nine days, with all the channels fighting for coverage of a single madrasa that had begun to serve as a metaphor for Pakistan's problems. Encouraged at first by the army, the radicalised extremists inside only became a problem when they began to act against their minders' wishes. They were tolerated when their entire output was Jihadist soldiers and anti-Indian rhetoric, but when they began dispensing vigilante justice on the streets of Islamabad – shutting down massage parlours and taking corrupt policemen hostage – they needed to be curbed. Many attempts were made at peaceful negotiations with the two brothers who ran the mosque and its adjoining women's madrasa, but all failed. So Musharraf once again turned to the strategy that had already failed him repeatedly in the past: the madrasa was put under siege.

For the next nine days, Pakistani television showed a continuous battle between militants inside the mosque and soldiers outside it. In the end, over 150 people died and many more were injured. Musharraf's final wisps of popularity dissipated with that attack. Even though it could be argued that the occupants were extremists, they were punished not for aiding terrorist groups but because they had shut down an illegal brothel running in the centre of the city under political patronage. Violent protests erupted across the country and there was a sharp increase in the frequency of suicide attacks.

The hours spent watching the Lal Masjid Siege through live feeds took its toll on all of us. One of the other producers began pouring whisky into his morning coffee, while an anchor took to taking alcohol breaks in the toilet between bulletins. I developed back and shoulder pains that even now flare up when I am confronted by stress; my wife told me I had begun talking in my sleep (apparently I was yelling 'cue' between snores, and demanding the reporter get me better footage).

Over the next few months, it got so that every time I walked into the office for my shift, regardless of what time of day it was, there was always some breaking news event unfolding. Bomb blasts, suicide attacks, gunfights, assassinations. These became so frequent that the stress of reporting them gave way to ennui. After a while, you stop being horrified by the state of affairs and start focusing on where the footage is for the 7 pm bulletin and why the anchor refuses to fix that cowlick sticking up from the back of his head.

Nevertheless, the pressures began to create cracks in the camaraderie we had all experienced until then. Fights erupted more frequently among editors and reporters, and the HR department had to issue warning letters with such frequency they eventually stopped bothering to put names on them. Most newsrooms have enough antagonism in them to create a noxious stench of rage. High pressure and bulging egos combine to erupt into a regular flurry of fists and improvised streams of cursing. It is the kind of environment that only a journalist feels relaxed in.

When, years later, I was given a tour of the Australian Broadcasting Corporation's Perth newsroom, I found the entire place disconcertingly peaceful. Everyone spoke in hushed tones and greeted each other with sincere politeness. It took all my self-control not to start swinging, just so I would feel more at ease.

--------- • ---------

Dawn News established itself as a respected name in television journalism in that first year. As Musharraf's authority collapsed with alarming speed and the ensuing destruction created opportunities for the return of exiled former politicians, we managed to provide several exclusive interviews with Benazir Bhutto, General Musharraf himself and other major players in the newly forming political landscape. Our reporters provided coverage of the same terrorist attacks as other channels but, whereas the others focused on the gory aftermath, we showed restraint and tried to focus on the repercussions instead of the body parts. It was the same philosophy of self-control that had earned the newspaper its enduring reputation. But then we were taken off the air.

The censorship wasn't limited to us. On 3 November 2007, Musharraf declared a state of emergency. The constitution was suspended; channels had their transmissions blocked and judges were placed under house arrest. In keeping with its tradition of poor timing, this was the same day Dawn News had chosen to finally host a dinner celebrating its earlier launch. Dressed formally, and eating plates of sushi that had been meant for the celebrities and politicians who never turned up, we watched as the screens went black.

However, we were still visible to viewers with access to satellite dishes and to foreign audiences who had tuned in to our international broadcast, so the next day we carried on working as though our national audience was still watching, even though it couldn't. We continued broadcasting into the ether for several weeks before being allowed back on the national airwaves. A few weeks after that I moved out of the news department, having lost my appetite for the news when I stepped out of an OB van on the night of Benazir Bhutto's arrival in Karachi.

7

The thing I remember most clearly was seeing a man's lungs on fire. I lunged out of the van with a cameraman right behind me, both of us running up the street and past the police cars and ambulances.

'No close-ups,' I yelled over the wailing of survivors.

There had been two bomb blasts. The brunt of the first was borne by the armoured bus carrying Benazir Bhutto. The thick iron shielding that had been welded to the sides of her vehicle saved Benazir Bhutto, who was able to escape out of a side hatch and was rushed away by her handlers. Unfortunately for the hundreds of people pressed against the bus, compacted tightly by their devotion to her, the force of the explosion ricocheted off the side and spread outwards, like water splashing against a wall.

Then, as the survivors staggered to their feet, trying not to slip and fall on the blood slick underfoot, a second suicide bomber threw himself into a police van parked nearby. This explosion carried not just heat and kinetic force but also thousands of ball bearings that had been stuffed inside the attacker's jacket. They sliced through anyone in their path before coming to a stop in the trees and cars nearby.

The death toll was 139 people, most of them shredded to bits right where they stood. Over 450 were injured. In both lists were men, women and children of all ages. The bus was a black husk, gutted by fire and smashed inwards by the force of the explosions. The road around it glistened with red pulp.

'I'm walking on people,' I remember thinking as every step squelched underfoot.

Azhar Abbas had given me my orders during our brief phone conversation – find Aftab Borka, our reporter colleague who had gone missing since the blast, find the cameraman, who had not been heard from either, and get footage and interviews. The cameraman accompanying me, who had already witnessed the aftermath of other explosions, whistled at the devastation and then began worrying about lighting and focusing.

I realised that searching for my missing colleagues would entail looking at the dead bodies strewn around, something I had managed to avoid in the first few minutes since leaving the van. That was when I looked down and saw the man with the burning lungs.

His face was completed melted away; his skin was liquefied, so it ran like wax off the muscle beneath. He wore jeans and a shirt. Amazingly his jeans, though blood-soaked down to the knees, were not torn and the shirt still had the sleeves buttoned at his wrists. I remember the black-and-white-checked pattern of that shirt. Below his neck, however, his chest had been blown open, as if a great gas bubble had burst out from under his breastbone. The ribs were shattered, edges jutting like broken fencing around a mess of cooked meat. I stopped and stared because, despite the black char of what must have been his heart, the lungs were still a fresh pink.

'How are his lungs still healthy?' I wondered.

Then I realised they were glowing, like coals in a fire. Their colour was not naturally rosy, but deepening into red, like steak when first put on a high heat. A single orange nail of flame poked through one lung, quivering in the evening breeze and then retreating back inside.

I don't know how long I stood there. Long enough for the cameraman who had accompanied me to come back and move me out of the way. Four men with a large blanket stretched between them were collecting body parts, the blanket sagging as it became weighted with arms, legs and scraps of flesh. They had been asking me to move for several seconds before the cameraman shook me.

I moved aside just quickly enough to avoid being pushed out of their way. I stumbled; then I sat down on the kerb and watched as they lifted a chunk of scalp off the ground, hair still matted across it, and tossed it into the blanket.

'Don't film them,' I said to the cameraman. 'We'll interview them when they're done.'

I got up and began looking for Aftab the reporter and Abid the missing camerman.

Abid had been close enough to the bus that, after the initial blast, he began running towards it – which was when the second explosion hit him. He was thrown to the ground, with shrapnel slicing into his legs and stomach. When we reached him, he was being loaded onto a stretcher, still conscious but barely coherent. While the cameraman with me returned to the task of aiming his lenses on the devastation, I helped the other volunteers lift Abid into the back of an ambulance. When the doors shut, I wiped my hands on my shirt, discovering it was already too damp with blood to be of any use in drying.

Still not seeing Aftab anywhere, I began to interview witnesses. Then, with no other option, I stood in front of the camera and prepared to give a live report to the studio about what I had seen. That's when we spotted Aftab. He was walking towards us, pale and shaking.

Later he told me how he had been on the bus minutes before the explosion, only climbing off because the cameraman had convinced him that they weren't getting any worthwhile footage from up there. 'I didn't want to get off but he convinced me.'

I remember feeling relieved. With a reporter and cameraman in place, I could be a producer, blocking out the traumatic visuals by focusing on the job I was trained to do. I calmed Aftab as best I could, and then stuck him in front of the camera.

Several hours later, with multiple tapes of footage having been beamed back to the office from our OB van, Aftab and the rest of the crew returned to the office, their replacements on the way to the scene. I walked home. The procession had been less than a kilometre from my house when it was attacked. My family had seen the light of both blasts shear the evening sky, the windows of the house trembling in their wake. I recall stopping once to look back at the rescue teams that had descended on the site and at the last of the bodies being carted away. Standing there, covered in the blood of other people, I had a single thought. Then I continued on my way.

When my wife opened the door, she started screaming. I had to reassure her that the blood wasn't mine. I stripped off my clothes in the bathroom, threw them in the garbage and stood under the shower for several minutes. Then I went to sleep.

--------- • ---------

The next day I returned to the office. We all did. There's no time for personal traumas in a breaking news environment. Even Aftab was there, although he admitted to me that he was no longer capable of reporting from places with large crowds – it unnerved him too much. For my part, I couldn't remember anything that I had seen the night before.

For a long time after, all I could see with any clarity was the man with the burning lungs. The rest was all black, like scenery in a photograph that has been chewed away by silverfish. The brain protects itself in whatever way it can; sometimes that means selectively editing out what is too traumatic to retain. It was only years later, when being interviewed for a documentary show in Australia, that I remembered the rest. The interviewer noted that, when pressed about what I might have seen, my only response was, 'I really don't remember much.' I said this over and over, like a mantra. She didn't push beyond that, but when she pointed it out to me, it made me curious about whether I actually could remember. And I slowly began unpacking the details of that night.

Sometimes I feel silly about my reaction. As though I'm making a bigger deal out of it than the incident warrants. Many Karachiites would agree. 'You didn't die,' they'd say, 'so get over it.' Trauma is a luxury Pakistanis have neither time for, nor the patience to process.

A couple of weeks later, Azhar promoted me from the control room to senior producer of current affairs. Over a year had passed since I had joined and he wanted to make space for newer panel producers to climb up into the seats vacated by the original three. Mikail was put in charge of the channel's flagship news analysis show, *News Eye*. Hosted by Saima Mohsin, a former BBC journalist, it is still spoken of with great respect. Sahar moved across to the news desk, where she served as news editor, using her laser-like brilliance to slice through hyperbole and pare every story down to its essence. I was handed *Breakfast at Dawn*.

Every news channel starts its morning with a breakfast show, in which two or more hosts ease the viewing audience into the day with a combination of light banter and sparkling personalities. Their goal is basically to give you just enough news for you to get caught up in it, but not so much as to spoil your appetite for cereal. However, we had a different idea at Dawn News. We decided that our breakfast show would set the news agenda for the day, so from 7 am to 9 am, two hosts would use research, informed guests and intelligent discussion to create a tone of journalistic seriousness that would then be transferred to the rest of the day's programming.

Anchoring the show were Faisal Qureshi and Ayeshah Alam. Faisal is a human Swiss Army knife – an entrepreneur, software developer, electrical engineer, founder of a non-profit organisation and host of several talk shows. He's the kind of guy who dresses up in police uniforms to secretly film people trying to bribe their way out of traffic violations and then chairs a Mensa meeting in the evening. Ayeshah is a former model who was briefly married to the bassist from Junoon, moved on to become a popular television actress, then got bored and reinvented herself as a documentarian and talk show host. They were both quick thinking, news obsessed and entirely too cheerful at 7 am for my liking.

The benefit of being the producer on the breakfast show was that every day started at 4 am and ended at 1 pm. No more rotating shifts meant that, for the first time in over a year, I could predict when I'd see family and friends again. I began to enjoy being a part of dinner plans and family get-togethers, and my wife and parents discovered that I did actually do more than just come home to sleep.

The downside of being the producer on the breakfast show, however, was that every day started at 4 am, which meant I woke an hour before the sun had even considered clawing its way up into the sky; I was showered, dressed and out of the door at 4.30. I have never functioned well in those early hours and the twenty-four-hour petrol station store on my route to work soon knew to have a chilled can of Red Bull ready for me at exactly 4.35 every morning.

By 5 am I was in the office dissecting the previous day's news, along with any late-night developments I might have missed. This involved scouring the Reuters and Associate Press feeds for footage and sound bites worth harvesting, watching several news reports from the day before to try to predict the way the news would develop for the next few hours, speed-reading the morning papers, both national and international, and then collating it all into a coherent script for the hosts to read and – if need be – improvise around.

By 6 am, Ayeshah and Faisal would arrive, have their makeup done and skim my notes; then, while they had chirpy conversations with the rest of the office staff, I tried to hide my bitterness at being forced to wake so early and began queuing up the footage and graphics. At 7 am the show started and my assistant producers efficiently moved a stream of guests and callers through the studio for Ayeshah and Faisal to scrutinise while I licked the top of the long-empty can of Red Bull. Once the show ended at 9 am, we would meet to discuss any ideas and then begin preparing for the next day's show. By 1 pm my head would start sagging; I'd answer any questions with a braying snore and be allowed to return home.

Producing the breakfast show was much less stressful than life as a panel producer, though, and I was grateful for the change – until 27 December 2007, at least.

With the New Year just around the corner, we had decided to prerecord the 1 January show so that both the hosts could enjoy New Year's Eve without having to worry about waking up early the next day.

'The year's almost over,' I remember saying. 'What else could possibly happen?'

On the afternoon of the twenty-seventh, we prerecorded the show – the only time we had ever done so – and then called it a day. As I left the office at around 6 pm, the news bulletin was showing a live broadcast of Benazir Bhutto delivering a speech to a crowd of supporters in Rawalpindi.

It took me forty minutes to reach home that day, which wasn't bad considering the rush-hour traffic. But during that time, in a park on the other side of the country, while the former prime minister of Pakistan was waving to her supporters from the sunroof of her truck, a fifteen-year-old boy had squeezed through the adoring crowds as her truck inched forward, pulled a gun out from under his jacket and fired three shots. Benazir Bhutto had collapsed inside the truck, which was rocked a moment later when the boy exploded, killing twenty-four other people as well.

I got home just in time to hear my mother yell out that Benazir was dead. Watching the TV, I saw the anchors repeating this statement with unquestionable finality: 'Benazir Bhutto is dead.'

The country rioted. In every major city, Benazir's supporters erupted in a frenzy of grief, leaving destruction in their wake. Shops were broken into, cars were burned, buildings torched and police attacked. Many abandoned their cars wherever they were, only to return later to find smoking wreckage. My wife wasn't home at the time, and being closer to her parents' house she took refuge there for the next two days. An American friend of ours, visiting Pakistan for the first time in a decade, spent those two days unable to leave the airport and eventually flew back out. By night the rioters would exhaust themselves and retreat, only to continue their miserable orgy of violence the next day. But at 4 am on the morning after Benazir's death, I left for work.

I drove through the city without headlights, using the illumination cast by burning cars and tyres to find my way past the orange bonfires raging against a bruised sky. Several times I had to take side streets because the main roads were too glutted with twisted metal and glowing rubber. I was, again, the only car moving on the roads at that time. When I got to the office, I discovered I was the first to arrive since the assassination had become official. Everyone who had been at work when it happened just stayed, while those who had left were unable to return.

By the time Ayeshah and Faisal were due in the studio, the rioting had resumed and they were unable to make it, so we used Ali Mustafa as our anchor instead. For four hours he single-handedly hosted the morning show, which served as the only bulletin until more people arrived, with me running the entire control room on my own.

Two hours into that sombre broadcast, Azhar Abbas pulled me aside and told me we had an exclusive that needed to run immediately. One of our reporters had received, from an anonymous source, the first photographs of the assassin. Sure enough, there were pictures showing a fair man (who later turned out to be a boy) wearing dark glasses and a black suit, pointing a gun at Benazir Bhutto from just a few feet away. It was the kind of photograph taken inadvertently, with the subject barely in the frame. It was also the photograph which made Dawn News known internationally, as every news channel around the world ran it with a 'Courtesy Dawn News' graphic plastered across it.

The next day, the government held a press conference and announced that Benazir hadn't died as a result of gunshot or explosion but by hitting her head on the sunroof lever. It was the fastest forensic analysis ever performed in Pakistan and the X-rays held up at the press conference were the only smidgen of evidence remaining from the attack, given that both the bombsite and the truck had been hosed down by police even before Benazir breathed her last.

--------- • ---------

After several days of frenzied activity, my job once again settled back into its familiar rhythms. I produced *Breakfast at Dawn* for a full year; any regret I felt at leaving the domain of the news bulletins was assuaged by seeing the toll it took on those still confined to it. Perhaps, in a more sedate news environment, it can be a long-term career. But the steadily growing atmosphere of violence in Pakistan ravages those whose job it is to catalogue that destruction. There's a reason why almost everyone who spends a career in the news is left with little hair, a steady smoking habit and almost no sense of humour.

That last was important to me: having a sense of humour. Confronted with the jagged edges of the world I was in, I was retreating more and more into the padded cell that comedy provides. This stemmed from the single thought I had had when staring at the carnage of the 18 October blast. I remember looking across at the grisly vista, my clothes soaked in blood, and thinking, 'I need to do comedy. The world can't be like this. I need to do comedy.'

I, COMEDIAN

8

Two minutes before my first stand-up comedy show, I vomited. Sitting backstage in the green room of a Karachi auditorium, I could hear the audience filling the hall just beyond the curtains; the expectant chatter of 200 people fusing into a continuous buzzing that seemed to vibrate through my intestines. My wife came into the small room, with its humming fluorescent light and its single rattling fan, and told me we were ready to start whenever I wanted.

'Are you okay?' she asked, noticing how my complexion had paled to that of parchment.

I tried to answer that I was fine, but instead bolted from my chair into the adjoining bathroom. I reached the toilet bowl just in time.

My wife waited patiently until I was done heaving, retching and generally sounding like a mule in the final stages of labour, and then she offered me a bottle of water. 'Are you sure you want to do this?' she asked.

I washed my face, put my spectacles back on and said, 'Yes,' with a great deal less confidence than I was hoping to muster.

'You'll be great,' she told me, kissing me despite my rancid breath. (Kissing someone whom you have just seen spewing violently has to be the most unquestionable evidence of love.) Then she grabbed the wireless microphone she had brought with her, flicked it on and made the announcement: 'Ladies and gentlemen,' her voice boomed through the speakers, instantly hushing the audience outside, 'please put your hands together for . . . Sami Shah!'

I took the microphone from her and walked out onto the stage as the curtains rose. A single spotlight glared at me so brightly I couldn't even see the people in the front row. There was a smattering of polite applause, followed by an audible intake of breath as 200 people crossed their arms and dared me to make them laugh. It was the first English stand-up comedy show in Pakistan, as well as the first time I had ever attempted stand-up comedy at all; I knew that if the first joke went badly, the next hour would be the most humiliating experience of my life.

'I love holidays,' I said, focusing on keeping the nervous stammer out of my voice. 'Holidays used to be a big deal when we were kids. I still love them, but back then it meant not only a day off but also new stuff to watch on TV. This was back when our viewing options were limited to PTV. Kids used to get four and a half minutes of *Heckle and Jeckle*, and then it would be interrupted by the news. For a long time I thought the prime minister's travel itinerary was an integral part of Heckle and Jeckle's adventures!'

They laughed. It was a big laugh – much bigger than the material warranted, I know now. Mostly it was a relieved laugh. It was far from the funniest thing they had ever heard, but it tugged at a shared childhood experience and exaggerated it enough to reassure them that I wouldn't be wasting the next hour of their time.

If that first joke had failed, I'd probably have never done stand-up comedy again. That it did work meant that, since then, whenever anyone asked me what I did professionally, I never answered with, 'Oh, I work in advertising,' or, 'I'm a news producer.' I always said, 'I'm a comedian.'

People outside Pakistan are always amazed when I tell them that Pakistan has a storied history of comedy – mostly because I use words like 'storied' superfluously. Also 'superfluously'. In fact, having a sense of humour is an inherent part of the national character. Even more integral than Pakistan's love of all things Islamic, its paranoia about American interests and its disturbing tolerance of extremist fundamentalism is its ability to find comedy in the blackest of darkness.

Even before the smoke has cleared from a tragedy, inappropriately hilarious jokes are shared about it. Foreigners might think this callous; a psychologist would say it is evidence of mass repression or perhaps a coping mechanism utilised when confronted by so much uncontrollable chaos and oppression. I've always believed it is evidence of the true irrepressibility of the Pakistani spirit. Dictators can crush our freedoms, endemic corruption can swallow our hopes and terrorists can end our lives, but we will continue to bare our teeth – not in a grimace but in a grin.

I became aware of the power of comedy as a child. The first decade of my life was lived during the height of Zia Ul Haq's military dictatorship. The reign of Pervez Musharraf, by comparison, was positively benign. Zia Ul Haq came to power in a coup in 1977, one year before I was born. By the time I was two, he had had the former prime minister of Pakistan, Zulfikar Ali Bhutto (Benazir Bhutto's father), hanged and was well into his eleven-year rule over the country.

During those eleven years, his fetish for conservative Islam and brutal intolerance of criticism fundamentally changed the country. Laws hostile to women were enacted, madrasas that taught the value of violent Jihad flourished and freedom of speech was mocked and then flogged in the streets. Journalists critical of his rule were punished publicly and women's rights activists baton-charged. The only television channel available to the country for viewing was PTV (Pakistan Television Corporation), which offered tightly regulated content under strict censorship guidelines.

But creativity always flourishes when it is most oppressed. Sitcoms and sketch comedy shows appeared on air, seemingly innocuous but riddled with double meanings and sly metaphors. Many of these were written and performed by a trio of comedic geniuses who did more to shape my own understanding of comedy than anyone else. Anwar Maqsood, a man with a gull's tail of white hair framing a deceptively serious face, was the writer of most of the shows. He presented dramas and talk shows that, on the surface, seemed simply patriotic and utterly domestic. It was only when I was much older that I realised how much acidic satire was being aimed at the military rulers in the guise of harmless comedy. His approach was perfectly encapsulated in his hosting style, the dry, halting delivery distracting from the sarcastic content. With him were Moin Akhter, an impersonator and mimic who could effortlessly parody any regional accent and stereotype, and Bushra Ansari, a talented comedian with a range of characters and voices at her command. Every time the three of them appeared on television, my family would gather around to laugh at their farcical ability and to marvel at the near-subliminal satire.

Alongside them, a sketch show called *Fifty-Fifty* with its own cast of comedic actors served up similarly critical messages frosted over with light-hearted hilarity. I watched all these shows as a child, oblivious to the hidden messages; I only appreciated them for their ability to make me laugh until I wept.

When I was six years old, I was forced to attend a family wedding in Lahore (anything I did at six that didn't involve playing with my toys or reading involved force). Once dinner had been served and the bride and groom duly fawned over, it was announced that Moin

Akhter had been hired to perform for the guests. Having done many comedy shows for money since then, I know from personal experience that there is nothing a comedian hates more than performing at a Pakistani wedding. It's frequently outdoors, the crowd is distracted, and after dinner everyone wants to go home. It's a terrible setting for live comedy, which makes the ease with which Moin Akhter controlled our every laugh all the more marvellous.

Excited at the prospect of seeing someone from TV actually perform in real life, I positioned myself right in front of the stage. Over the next hour, I got to watch him transform from character to character with just a hunch of the shoulder or adjustment of the accent, all with a rapid-fire delivery. His big closer for the night was acting like the singer of a hit pop song who gets more and more exhausted by his own success as the audience keeps forcing him into an encore. By the end, the song's lyrics are whimpered and the singer is full of bitterness and pain.

My family was hysterical with laughter, barely being able to gasp out the demand that the 'singer' perform 'Once more! Once more!'

I, however, was horrified. Utterly believing in the character being portrayed, I felt sorry for him and began to add my own, more sympathetic, cry to the crowds'. 'No more!' I yelled. 'No more!' I just wanted the poor singer to get a moment's respite. (In retrospect, I also wanted to be noticed for my compassion and appreciated for it – demonstrating a mix of sincerity and egotism that all but guaranteed me my own future in comedy). For a brief moment, though, as quick as a whisper, Moin Akhtar broke character, crouched down and told me, 'Don't worry, son, it's all an act. They love it.'

Then, before anyone else caught that moment between us, he was back up, whimpering and mewling as his character responded to the crowd's insatiable demands.

My mind was blown. Comedy, he showed me, was performance. It also, most importantly, asked for commitment. It didn't matter if you were appearing on stage or on a television show, where the audience was there to laugh, or at a wedding, where they had grudgingly torn themselves away from the food line. All that mattered was that you brought your confidence and enthusiasm to the act. If you did that, your audience would laugh at you, for you. It was the first lesson in comedy I ever received and is probably still the most important one.

9

The first time I did comedy, it was for a girl.

Isn't that always the case? Most comedians will claim they do what they do because they are compelled to satirise the world around them, to use their warped sensibilities to make sense of reality, perhaps even to mine the depths of self. But more often than not, it's because they think it will impress someone.

In my case, it all started in January 2003, when I had just returned to Karachi from the US. Faris, an old friend of mine from high school, invited me to watch the debut performance of an improvisational comedy troupe he had joined.

'What's improvisational comedy?' I asked.

'Like *Whose Line is it Anyway?*' Faris said. 'We take audience suggestions then improvise comedy around them. It's really difficult, but fun.'

'I always thought that stuff was just fake – you know, that they rehearsed it all.'

'Nope. There are rehearsals – we've been rehearsing for six months for our first show – but that's all about learning to think quickly and using certain structures to make everything, like, coherent while also being funny. Come check it out. It's not like there's anything else to do.'

He was right. Karachi had little entertainment to offer and I was already bored. So I went along.

Black Fish was founded by Saad Haroon. The son of an industrialist, Saad chose to dodge a future of managing his father's factories and instead dedicate himself to comedy. Having spent his college years in America hanging around comedians and improv troupes, he came back with an understanding of the work involved in being funny and a desire to spread that comedic germ. He recruited seven other like-minded people through extensive auditions and then taught them the tools needed to perform short-form improv. Their first show was held in the basement of a cafe, with a small audience of friends in attendance.

I expected it to be terrible, but for half an hour the troupe of amateur improv comedians filled the high-ceilinged room with laughter. Dressed in blue jeans and identical black t-shirts emblazoned with the white Black Fish logo, they effortlessly transformed audience suggestions into stream-of-consciousness hilarity. Saad served as the master of ceremonies, exhibiting a contagiously frenetic energy as he bounced across the room coaxing suggestions out of the shy audience and then bringing pairs of improvisers on stage to perform comedic games around those suggestions. If it looks rehearsed and scripted, that means it's working; improv is successful when it seems too good to be improvised.

I watched the entire performance alternating between guffaws and wide-eyed wonder. I also experienced slack-jawed awe. That last was directed not at the performances but at a girl in the troupe.

Ishma Alvi was one of the founding members of Black Fish. At high school she had been a year above me and so one of those girls I stared at longingly while acknowledging how utterly unattainable she was. Back then, she used to have a mass of thick curls streaming down her back and a brooding intensity that drew me like a moth to an extremely sexy flame. I didn't see her after she graduated and it took a few seconds for me to recognise the tall, slim girl with close-cropped hair on stage.

After the show, I went up to Faris and gushed about how amazing the entire troupe was. We walked out onto the street, where the rest of the audience was already reminiscing about the shared experience. As I was about to ask Faris about Ishma, she came bounding up.

'Sami! Hi! Faris told me you were back from America. It's great to see you!' she said, throwing her arms around me.

'Blurble huggle ung bleck,' I replied. (I wish I was exaggerating, but the truth is I tried to say something smart and clever and complimentary, and that was all that came out.)

Ishma, understandably, gave a slightly confused smile; then she high-fived Faris and went off.

'What the fuck was that, man?' Faris asked, laughing.

'I need to join your troupe,' I said.

--------- • ---------

A few weeks later, I was invited to attend my first rehearsal. Black Fish rehearsed twice a week, every week. Each rehearsal lasted two hours and attendance was mandatory if you wanted stage time at the Sunday performance. Rehearsals weren't, as many assumed, about trying to anticipate every possible audience suggestion. That is impossible, even if most times audience suggestions never stray much further than 'my uncle' and 'cats.' Improvisational comedy relies on certain rules and we practised the application of those rules. The most important one is 'Yes, And' – the idea being that, no matter what is said to you by either an audience member or another performer, you should agree with it and then expand on it.

For example, the audience suggestion for a scene might be 'A surgeon and a twelfth-century blacksmith walk into a disco'. Faris, assuming the role of the surgeon, would turn to me and say, 'My God, I haven't heard this song in forever. Don't you just love it? I just spent four hours elbow-deep in spleen, let's dance!' At this point, given that I have been cast as the twelfth-century blacksmith, I need to respond in a manner appropriate to my character, agreeing with his statement and then progressing the scene. So I try to 'Yes, And' him by saying, 'Indeed! Verily these sounds remindeth me of the same sounds created when I bash metal into shape over my fire with a heavy hammer. Pray tell, what may be the name of this infernal music?' Which then sets Faris up to reply, 'Heavy metal.' Cue laughter. Or groans. Sometimes groans work just as well.

The other law of improv is 'Advance and Expand'. Advancing is when you develop whatever story is being played out on stage. Expanding is when you develop the imaginary environment you are inhabiting. If this all sounds tremendously boring, then that's because the nuts and bolts of comedy usually is. Any fool can make people cry. Making them laugh is serious business and hard work.

Rehearsals were rotated around everyone's houses, with the entire troupe meeting at 8 pm for rigorous training conducted by Saad. Along with Saad, Faris, myself and Ishma, there was Umar Rana, a bald and astoundingly sweaty banker by day, who saw every conversation as a battle which he could only win by being the loudest; Yasser Salehjee, an architect with a ponytail and an innate understanding of physical comedy, able to bend and contort his body like an Olympic-level stripper with missing vertebrae; Sanam Saeed, a high school student with far more confidence on stage than is probably healthy; and Cyrus Viccajee, a short, half-Parsee, half-Christian art student with a tendency to turn even the most mundane scene into something stupefyingly surreal. In the years since Black Fish disbanded, almost everyone in the troupe has gone on to do something performance-related with a great deal of success. Saad and I became stand-up comedians; Faris and Sanam have acted in theatre and TV dramas, with the latter currently being one of Pakistan's most renowned young actresses; Umar runs a comedy club in Singapore; and Cyrus teaches improv at a drama school in Karachi.

There have been improv troupes in Pakistan since Black Fish, but none have been as popular or as effortlessly hilarious as the original. Whenever we tried incorporating more people into the troupe, we discovered it just didn't work. Our sensibilities all connected too tightly for some indefinable reason. Sometimes the right people just happen to come together at the right time.

My only interest in the first few weeks of rehearsal was, of course, Ishma. Courting someone is strange when you're doing comedy together. The more traditional approach is dependent on both people spending the first few meetings trying to convince each other how utterly perfect they are. You are smart and witty, dress in your best clothes and try to walk like a movie star when you enter a room, before laying down a bit of revelatory exposition. The idea is that if you look, sound and smell fantastic, the other person will be fooled into thinking you are that amazing all the time. It's kind of difficult to pull that off, however, when three times a week you have to behave like an utter imbecile.

At rehearsals and on stage, we had to surrender our egos entirely to the demands of comedy. That means acting silly, saying the most ridiculous things possible and generally behaving like clue-less buffoons. Somehow, it helped. I was never particularly good at constructing the artificial persona required of most first interactions and Ishma seemed to find my ability to be funny more attractive than any lame attempt I might have made to appear cool.

Which isn't to say it was easy. Asking girls out was never something I was particularly good at, and I had a fairly poor success rate. As a result, I basically never did it. Like all insecurities, this one stemmed from childhood trauma – in my case, from the first rejection I ever suffered.

Her name was Soha, and in seventh grade she was the most beautiful girl I had ever seen. Until the end of sixth grade she had been as androgynous as every other girl in our class. After the summer holidays, however, when all the girls disappear for three months to cocoon themselves inside pink bedrooms, she emerged with breasts and makeup. Soha was my sun and my moon, my stars and my skies; her very existence was evidence to me of a Greater Being, who loved beauty. In retrospect, she was probably a pimply girl with bad hair, braces and terrible posture, but given that I was a pimply boy with bad hair, thick spectacles and terrible posture, I wasn't in any position to be too discerning.

Every day I would sit two rows behind her in class and ignore the teacher's lessons, busily concocting scenarios in which the beautiful Soha would find herself in danger, surrounded on all sides by men with vile intentions, perhaps in a dark alleyway. Her cries for help are ignored by the indifferent residents of the apartment blocks that tower on each side, blotting out all light and hope. One of those men confronting her, his hand caked with the blood of earlier victims, reaches for her; his crooked yellow teeth bare in a smile that reveals his deviant plans. He begins to laugh as she presses up against the wall in fear. Then he screams in pain.

The hand that was reaching for her is twisted in a way that defies anatomy. The space between him and her is now occupied – by me.

The balcony I dropped from still hums like a tuning fork. He falls backwards as she gasps my name.

His minions charge, roaring their surprise and rage. I sidestep neatly, grabbing the nearest one by his lapel and using his momentum to change his course, smashing him into the hard brick wall. His nose flattens with a satisfying crunch. Then the third attacker is upon me. As he swings a fist at my face, I turn my head slightly, letting it fly uselessly past. I counter with an elbow that smashes his teeth, and then a fist that dislocates his jaw. The defeated vermin slink away, leaving Soha and me alone in that alleyway.

I calm myself, letting the adrenaline rush subside. Summoning up something cool to say, I turn to her. Her straight black hair frames a perfect face; large eyes stare back at me.

'Thank you,' she says, and then: 'You saved me.'

'It was nothing,' I reply, pulling her closer. Then she kisses me. I kiss her back . . .

For almost a full year, I spent hours every day coming up with scenarios much like this one. Soha, for her part, either didn't know I existed or didn't care. A more confident individual than me would have simply asked her out. Maybe after first initiating a conversation peppered with compliments and self-effacing charm that would leave her intrigued. I was then, and am now, utterly incapable of such a bold move.

It took a full year of circling her like an insecure shark before I finally walked up to her one day and said: 'I know we haven't spoken much ever, but I think you would really lo—like me . . . if you got to know me. Because I really lov—like you. A lot. So what do you think?'

It was the bravest thing I had ever done – braver than any act of heroism performed throughout the ages. I was not the first man to love, nor will I be the last. History has recorded countless poetic expressions of love; my humble offering will probably not find a permanent place in the historical record. Future generations may not quote it and writers may not wish they had thought of it, but it got the point across.

Her response was seven words long. Seven words that tore my heart out of my chest and threw it to the floor, where it lay beating in a pool of black blood. Seven words that are the cruellest thing any woman has ever said to a man. Each word was, on its own, harmless. But together . . . oh, together they hurt. They killed.

She turned to me and, with the smile of an executioner before swinging the axe, said: 'I think of you like a friend.'

Like a friend. There is no crueller hell. I wanted to say, 'No, damn you! I already have friends! I don't need any more!'

It's not like I was asking for much. This was seventh grade in a mediocre private school in Karachi. Dating meant you sat together during the lunch break and shared a plate of biryani. Nothing more. I wasn't asking for anything that would be too demanding of her physically or mentally. And how could she think of me 'like a friend' if the only conversation we'd ever had before this was two years earlier, when she asked me for a pencil sharpener?

I do not know why this first rejection so affected my ability to approach women from then on. I knew plenty of boys who took rejection after rejection, yet kept on rolling their hopeful rock of appeals back up the hill. But not me. After that, I never asked anyone out. Traumatised, I could feel the sting of rejection even before I had asked the question. This makes me all the more grateful to the women who decided to take the initiative. If it wasn't for the fact that they subsequently punched my heart with the force of Van Damme executing the Dim Mak on an innocent brick in *Blood Sport*, I would still remember those women fondly.

I met Meha during my first year in college. She sat next to me at Karachi airport and had asked me to kiss her by the time the flight landed in Washington DC. Four years older than me, she lived in Chicago, more than a thousand kilometres away from Virginia. In six months, we spent just a single weekend together. Then she moved to England, explaining that what she felt for me wasn't strong enough to compete with the job offer she had received. Tiffany, a drama major I met during my third year at university, pursued me with the single-minded zeal of a serial killer and then cheated on me with the man she went on to marry.

The years between and after those two women were filled with cigarette smoke, dreary songs on loop and lots of black clothes. I was still too frightened to take the initiative with a girl myself, and as a result I had been single for three years before I met Ishma.

Under the pretext of wanting to watch my *Six Feet Under* DVD set, Ishma began coming over to my house. Several times a week, we would sit together in my room and watch episodes on my computer. The only physical contact we had was when our hands brushed as we reached for the popcorn.

I was convinced that Ishma really liked *Six Feet Under* and she was convinced I was the strangest, most insecure man she had ever met. It turns out only one of us was right. Six episodes in, she finally turned to me and demanded: 'So are you ever going to kiss me, or what?'

I tried to play it as cool. With a wink and a smile, I replied, 'Actually, I was going to do it right now.' Then I pulled off my glasses, lost my vision entirely and kissed her chin.

Of course, inside my head there were trumpets going off and trapeze artists somersaulting through the air while streamers and confetti rained down on cheering crowds. Still, I think I played it pretty well.

We went on our first proper date the next day. Karachi marches on its stomach and so there is a veritable cornucopia of restaurants to choose from. We settled on a French bistro, where I failed a show of sophistication by attempting the French pronunciations when I ordered, before accepting defeat and just pointing to the dishes on the menu. After dinner, we went to a second-hand bookshop, partly as a way of spending more time together and partly to see which books the other gravitated towards. You can tell everything about a person by the books they read. If Ishma squealed and clapped her hands over *The Da Vinci Code*, I would probably have had to rethink my attraction towards her. She, no doubt, had similar concerns.

In the world of fantasy literature, there are two tiers of expertise. Most aficionados of that genre will salute *Lord of the Rings* as the greatest work of fantasy ever written. It's a reasonable assessment, of course. Most modern fantasy fiction can be traced back to Tolkien's influence, which is why dragons, orcs and elves are such common tropes. And even if one cannot suffer through the genealogies of Middle Earth's flora and fauna as excruciatingly detailed in the second book, there is no denying the epic scope of the trilogy. But the truly devoted adherents of the genre know that while *Lord of the Rings* is the foundation of modern fantasy, it's not the best book ever written in that category. That honour falls to the tragically overlooked and terminally ignored *Gormenghast* series by Mervyn Peake. Peake completed three books detailing the grey lives of characters living in the gothic Castle Gormenghast, dying of Parkinson's before he could write more than a few pages of the fourth book. It is a series devoid of magic, dragons or any creatures with pointy ears, pointy toes or pointy tails. Peake's prose is utterly lugubrious and reading it can be an oppressive experience that leaves you gasping for sunlight. And the whole thing is a marvellous achievement of imagination and characterisation.

The second-hand bookshop we were courting our way through had the entire trilogy collected in a single volume, and Ishma and I spotted it at the same time. We squealed identically and almost slapped each other's hands trying to be the first to grab it.

'I've read these so many times that my copies are completely falling apart,' Ishma said.

If I'd had a ring on my person, I would have proposed to her there and then. Even though it took a few weeks more before I formally asked her to marry me, my decision was made in that bookstore, standing in front of Mervyn Peake.

Our mothers, in whom we had both confided our feelings, were thrilled that we had decided to get married. Our fathers were more traditional and so needed to be granted the illusion of having some semblance of control over our lives. Arranged marriage isn't so much a custom in South Asia as a rigid belief system. Within that belief system, everyone involved is assigned a role; the mother chooses her child's spouse, the father approves of the choice, the child is informed of the final decision and allowed some input – but not too much, because children are generally stupid and shouldn't be allowed to make such monumental decisions on their own. In the urban upper and middle classes, arranged marriages have begun to decrease in recent years, but that change has only been acknowledged reluctantly by the older generations. Both our fathers knew we had been dating prior to our engagement, but we nevertheless went through the rituals of an arranged marriage. My mother told my father I had chosen 'that Ishma girl who he is friends with' for a bride and Ishma's mother told Ishma's father 'that Sami boy who comes around now and then would like to propose to Ishma'.

Our families met, discovered neither was abhorrent or criminal and actually got along quite well, and a wedding date was agreed upon. A small engagement ceremony was held at Ishma's house, attended by close relatives. The two of us, just returned from Black Fish rehearsals, exchanged engagement rings – and just like that, our lives were coiled together.

Pakistani weddings are extravagant affairs with enough pomp and pageantry to make a Roman triumphal march seem low-key in comparison. It took a full year of preparation for the wedding, during which time I discovered that the groom is actually the least important part of the entire proceedings. All the attention and focus is on the bride, the venue, the menu, the bride, the dowry and the bride. My turning up at the relevant time on the relevant day was basically all that was required of me.

Our wedding, like most Pakistani weddings, was stretched over four days. Day one was the Mehndi, when the two sides face off in near-violent dance battles of military precision, requiring hours of rehearsal. Although my brother and sister made a valiant showing of it, Ishma's sister was a seasoned veteran whose expertise was often sought after by friends and associates for whipping their own Mehndi dancers into competitive shape. As Ishma and I sat side by side, her face hidden under a yellow shawl, our siblings and their friends waged pitched battle in the form of twirls, gyrations and foot stomps. Meanwhile, an endless parade of relatives came up to us and took it in turns to stuff fistfuls of chocolate and desserts into our mouths until we both nearly fainted from early-onset diabetes. Eventually, as the night wore on, the dancers dragged the two of us onto the dance floor as well, then our parents and even our grandparents. Pretty soon, a few hundred people were stomping and bumping well into the night.

The next morning, those same people dragged themselves out of bed to attend the Nikah, the ceremony in which the marriage is legally and spiritually formalised. This was probably the most contentious part of the wedding, as traditionally a cleric oversees the entire service. Ishma's family was Sunni and mine was Shia, which meant there was a great deal of debate in the months leading up to the wedding as to which branch of Islam the cleric who heard our oaths would belong. In the end, a compromise was reached, the decision made easier by the fact that the bride and groom do the relevant oath-taking separately, meeting only once everything is signed. Ishma took her oaths in front of a Sunni cleric and I took mine in front of the Shia.

With the marriage legalised, we then parted ways only to meet again in the evening at the Shaadi. A more formal affair than the Dionysian Mehndi of the night before, the Shaadi required us both to sit serenely on stage as extended family posed for group photos around us. The evening ended with Ishma officially leaving her parents' home for mine, a departure marked with much weeping from her side of the family (my mother also cried, mostly because she never lets an opportunity to vent her tear ducts go to waste). I don't do well around crying people and instantly began to feel guilty and apologetic for depriving her parents of their beloved daughter. 'She can stay with you and I will visit every day,' I offered as her father wept on my shoulder.

There was one final event to power through; the Valima is a formal banquet in which the bride and groom sit and watch everyone they've ever known eat dinner. Officially it is a celebration of the consummation, but people try to avoid pointing that out because it makes for awkward dinner conversation. (This didn't stop at least one distant relative of mine coming up to us and proclaiming we looked different already, 'Because the hormones change after marriage yes?' Both our jaws hit the ground in unison.)

Finally, with the entire wedding over and everyone looking and feeling several years older, the two of us retired to the hotel suite we had been gifted for the night, where all our friends descended to help unravel Ishma from the several miles of shawl she had been mummified in for the evening. The next day we would fly off to our honeymoon in Thailand, where we looked forward to spending time alone for a couple of weeks, sipping drinks on the beach and dancing every night.

Except the next morning I woke up and turned on the TV to see the hotel we had booked for our honeymoon floating away on CNN. The 2004 tsunami had swallowed half the Indian Ocean coastline. Realising it would be poor form to complain about a missed holiday while so many suffered so much loss, we put off our honeymoon trip for six months and extended our stay at the Karachi hotel for a couple of nights. It didn't matter. All that did matter was that we were married. Two days later, when Ishma and I began our married life together, she brought the copy of *Gormenghast* I had bought for her.

10

A friend of mine once told me that the first time he smoked a cigarette, at the age of sixteen, it felt like feeding a craving he'd never realised he had. The sensation of nicotine passing over his tongue was strangely familiar, as if it was something he had always needed, but he'd never known it.

I can't remember the first time I made someone laugh, but it must have made a profound impression on me because, the first time I did something funny on stage with Black Fish, the laughter of the audience felt familiar and welcoming. I still remember it, a decade later.

The challenge for all the performers on stage was to come up with an example of The World's Worst something. In this case, the audience suggestion was The World's Worst Rapper. When it was my turn, I took a step forward and began miming. The world's worst rapper was mute. You had to be there, I guess. A hundred people roared in unison and I felt at home.

There is something terribly addictive about eliciting laughter intentionally – at least, if you have the correct alchemical mix of insecurities, hunger for validation and inflated egotism that marks most comedians. All of which, coincidentally, are qualities I possess.

That first crowd laugh filled me with pride. It was a hundred people coming together in agreement that something I had done caught them all by surprise, was something they would not have thought of doing, and they complimented me with their laughter and applause.

Even now, after a decade of doing comedy on stage, whenever I create moments of laughter with just the power of my own words and actions, nothing beats that feeling. For however long I own my audience's reactions, I feel as though I could do anything. I can kiss a nun and make her pregnant; I can beat a man thrice my size with a knuckle and an eyebrow; I can stitch the hole in the ozone layer with a rusty needle and a bit of string. And I can do all this while shading the world with my immense phallus. That's why I keep going back on stage.

I think, if you have to analyse it, it stems from narcissism. Being a narcissist means believing the whole world is thinking about you. The problem is that when you couple it with a deep-rooted insecurity like mine, you end up as a paranoid narcissist. I believe the whole world is talking about me – and no one is saying anything nice. Now you would think that I would therefore resist going on stage in front of large crowds and opening myself up to more scrutiny. But, in my head, I'm thinking the whole world hates me, but at least they're thinking about me. It's like being addicted to someone coming over every day and kicking you in the testicles. Yes, it hurts – but at least you had some company for a while.

From the first show, Black Fish was a success. Pakistanis were still optimistic in early 2003 and that first year of weekly shows reflected their appetite for frivolity. Doomsday politics had not yet begun to dominate the national discourse and so even our comedy was light-hearted.

There are no comedy clubs in the country and even a city as large as Karachi lacks adequate performance spaces. As the audiences grew, we moved out of the tiny thirty-seater basement and began searching for larger venues. For several months we did our show in a repurposed conference room attached to a shopping mall; then, when that closed, we relocated to an expensive auditorium which gave us a good deal since we were the only consistently booked act in the city.

Our audiences grew and we became a familiar part of Karachi's entertainment scene. We even developed a small but dedicated fan base – most notably, a British diplomat and his wife who attended every show we ever did. We thanked them with a lifetime free pass.

In 2004, we were invited by the British Council to a theatre festival in Manchester. The only catch was we had to produce a scripted performance. It was a booking I still can't quite make sense of – it was like hiring jazz musicians and then asking them to play only three-chord waltzes. Still, it isn't every day that you're offered a visa to the UK, free plane tickets and a week of hanging out with other theatre troupes from around the world.

Saad and I took up the challenge of scripting something that combined our improvisational abilities with the more traditional structure of a play. For a month, we met almost every day and banged out multiple drafts of a script that used everyone and conformed to the rules of the festival. In the end, we triumphantly emerged with a Joseph Campbell-esque mono-myth, by way of *Whose Line is it Anyway?* A hero, confronted by a world torn apart by war and strife, sets out to find companions in his quest to bring laughter to everyone, but each potential companion must first prove their comedic skills – at which point we would break from the script and erupt into a quick improv game that involved the audience. With each added member, the games grew larger, until the play ended with eight Black Fish members on stage, wildly improvising to shouted audience suggestions.

In Manchester, performing to an audience composed entirely of thespians from as far afield as Bangladesh and Scotland, we got two standing ovations and were the toast of the festival. If it sounds like I'm bragging, I am a little. Up until that moment, we never knew if we were genuinely any good.

In many ways, Pakistan is very isolated. Even when the world's cameras are all trained on the country and you can't toss a sound bite without hitting a dozen foreign journalists, all the attention is focused on one theatre of action; if it isn't related to terrorism, no one is interested.

The Middle East had that market cornered for most of the latter half of the last century (with the Venezuelans making a respectable bid for the title in the 1970s with Carlos the Jackal). For a very long time, though, it seemed like Arabs were the Apple computers of terrorism: they exported both quantity and quality. When James Cameron finally recognised their efforts by casting generic Arabs as troublemakers in *True Lies*, the rest of the world thought the game was over – the gold medal for mayhem had gone to the Middle East.

Then, like Usain Bolt breaking his own record, the Arab world produced Osama bin Laden. He became an overnight sensation. Soon teens with terrorist aspirations had his poster up on their walls and his audio and video releases topped the intelligence community charts. The sinister Saudi combined charisma with wealth, American CIA training with Afghan tenacity. He turned the whole terrorism industry upside down, transforming it from a bloated bureaucracy rife with nepotism into a twenty-first century open-source meritocracy.

September 11 was his Sistine Chapel. Any reasonable terrorist would have looked at that and admitted defeat.

But we Pakistanis pride ourselves on our lack of reason. Our terrorists worked harder – long hours, terrible working conditions, constant travel, drone attacks and a Pakistani government that treated them with all the consistency of a schizophrenic with multiple-personality disorder. Yet they persevered. And it paid off. With training institutes that churned out graduates who always made their instructors explode with pride, and celebrity terrorists like Baitullah Mehsud, who could return from the dead and show a disregard for civilian casualties that would make American presidents envious, we had finally arrived. By 2005, if you wanted to be respected as a terrorist, you had better be from Pakistan. The first question asked after any terrorist attack became, 'Is he Pakistani?' That's an achievement.

But in all the other fields of creative expression – theatre, music, art – we had no barometer of success. All we had was our own judgment and the patronage of an audience with severely limited entertainment choices. So when an auditorium full of international thespians stood up in ecstatic applause – not once, but twice – we felt as though we had been truly validated. Black Fish wasn't just good by Pakistani standards – it was good by any standard. We felt like rock stars, like movie stars, like Nobel laureates. Then we went back to our day jobs.

Even at the height of our success, we never made enough money to consider making Black Fish a full-time job. It never even became a consideration. The lack of choice in performance venues meant that most of our earnings were spent paying for the auditorium. Then there was the cost of the generator, to guarantee uninterrupted electricity throughout the show, not to mention the bribes needed to guarantee the police would stop the audience's cars from being stolen. It all added up.

So we all had real jobs. Faris and I worked together at the ad agency, and soon grew accustomed to the incongruity of signing autographs and being hailed as comedic geniuses in the evenings while filling out mind-numbing timesheets and bowing to client demands on the latest advertising campaign during the day.

As Black Fish grew in popularity, we began booking shows outside Karachi. Often we would leave work at 5 pm, catch a 6 pm flight to Lahore or Islamabad, perform a show, spend the night at a hotel, then take the 5 am flight back to Karachi and show up at work on time with our eyes only slightly swollen. The sheer joy that came from doing comedy was constantly dampened by the inanity of our day jobs, particularly for me, given how much I hated working in advertising. We envied comedians in America and England, who could earn enough from their craft not to need an office job. They were free to be who they really wanted to be, while we could only do it as a hobby.

Black Fish had a great run. For four years, we performed almost every week to sold-out audiences. In between there were corporate bookings that took us on nationwide tours and we even almost got our own TV show a few times. In the end, however, the troupe dispersed. Faris and Yasser moved to Dubai, Sanam left for college, Cyrus and I joined Dawn News and found our free time strangled, Umar Rana was relocated to Singapore by his bank and Ishma was concentrating on a master's degree.

Saad started another troupe, but it never really took off. Cyrus, too, gave it a shot and had the same disappointing result. Recreating that cohesion, which had occurred entirely by luck, proved impossible. To this day people in Karachi recognise most of us not from any of the TV appearances or stand-up comedy shows or anything else we might have done since, but from those four years in Black Fish.

For me, however, the end of Black Fish posed a unique problem. Like an addict, I needed my fix of validating laughter. I considered starting my own troupe, but I saw the failures encountered by the others and decided instead to try it alone. So, in 2005, I became a stand-up comedian.

11

Stand-up comedy is the purest of the performance arts. For a stand-up comedian, there is just a microphone and the audience. Musicians have their songs and it doesn't matter if there is one person listening or five hundred, the song remains the same. In a band the musicians even have each other to turn to for support, the same way improv comedians can find safety in the numbers that make up their troupe. When a joke fell flat in improv comedy, I could just take a step back and let someone else pick up the baton. Even stage plays have their script to hide behind, along with the props, other actors and the director's vision. If you fail in any of these performances, you can shift the blame, or thin the pain by spreading it around, or just continue on to the next tune, regardless of how the audience feels about it.

Stand-up comedians have none of those luxuries. If a joke fails, it's still just you up there and all you have is the fervent hope that the next one will work. As a stand-up comedian, on stage, you are presenting all of yourself. What you say starts in your brain and comes out of your mouth, and it is all you. The audience reaction is instant, for better or worse; and if they don't like what you're saying, it means, in a very direct way, that they don't like you. Which is why there is a prescribed route to becoming a stand-up comedian. If you wish to try becoming one – perhaps you too suffer from the toxic blend of paranoid insecurity and hunger for validation that can only be fed by large groups of people laughing at you – then the first thing to do is write something funny. Maybe on a computer or your phone, on a notepad or a post-it note. Or, if you are particularly pretentious, you get a Moleskine. You write a funny anecdote or observation, and that becomes your 'bit'. Then you find an open-mic night in the city you live in, perhaps at a coffee shop or a comedy club. Sometimes those open-mic nights can be a free-for-all, with musicians, poets and comedians all taking turns to hone their art in front of an audience of other amateur musicians, poets and comedians.

Many open-mic nights, however, are specific to one genre and you end up on stage in front of a small crowd of other comedians with a few actual civilians mixed in, often there because they misunderstood what was happening or are just too drunk to leave. Then you perform your bit. If the bit goes well, or 'kills', you start work on a new bit and return with that. If it goes badly, or 'bombs', you go home, cry into your pillow and consider the level of commitment you have to becoming a stand-up comedian.

There is a reason why the language is so extreme when referring to how a bit does on stage. When it lands successfully, the feeling of control and power you have over the audience is so immense you do indeed feel as though you could kill all of them with a wave of your hand. It's why comedians can be so brutal in dealing with hecklers – their sense of self is overinflated by their comedic ability and they are able to fell even the most drunken and loutish Goliath with a well-flung barb.

If, however, the joke falls flat, the thud of its collision with the floor echoing in the silence, then the audience reaction is very much like having a bomb detonate in the room. They recoil in horror and even the other comedians try to distance themselves from the failure in their midst, lest one of his flailing limbs crashes into them.

The harshness of this experience becomes apparent the first time a hopeful comedian steps up on stage. Bomb or kill, it takes a great leap of self-confidence to return. Most don't. Those who do, however, then begin working on more bits. Once you have enough bits to fill ten minutes or more, that becomes a 'set'. If your set succeeds in creating laughter more times than it fails, you might get a spot as a support act, meaning you get paid to be a comedian. It's not much – in fact it's usually barely anything at all – but it's still more than you were getting as an open-mic-er (which was absolutely nothing).

As a support act you hone your craft further. The material you write and then say out loud to audiences is just one aspect of being a stand-up comedian. There is also the delivery, which is how much stress you put on your words and where the pauses go and how each punch line is emphasised (this can be anything from a rise in volume to pulling your penis out on stage – I've seen both done effectively), and your stage persona. That last comes with time.

For the first few years, you will struggle to find your own unique personality while performing. This can be as elaborate as wearing a costume or behaving like you suffer from a mental disability to something as simple as talking faster or behaving more confidently than you normally do. In the end, every comedian comes to the same discovery – that the distance between who you are off stage and who you are on stage should be minimal. Slowly, as your set builds and your ability becomes more defined, you move up to MC (responsible for warming up the audience, introducing the support acts and being reliably funny enough to recover the crowd from any bombs). Finally, if you stick with it long enough and become good enough, you are the headliner.

The headliner is where the money is (still not much, but significantly more than the supports and infinitely more than the open-mic-ers). It also means you have to fill a minimum of forty-five minutes of stage time while holding the audience's attention and keeping them laughing throughout. If, as a headliner, you develop a sizeable fan following and become successful enough to sell tickets just on the strength of your name, then you ditch the rest of the gang, book a theatre and start doing an hour-long show all by yourself.

Stand-up comedy is one of the world's only true meritocracies. It takes years of hard work and training to achieve competence, and every comedian in the world will tell you the system exists the way it does because it needs to.

And that makes the way I started doing stand-up extremely stupid. The first time, I performed for an hour in front of 200 people. This wasn't due to bravado – there just weren't any open-mics in Pakistan in 2005. There are now, with every major city hosting at least a couple on a monthly basis, but in 2005 my only avenue for testing written material was my own judgment.

In my defence, I did try to learn the craft. I sought out comedy albums by the biggest names in stand-up – Jerry Seinfeld, Robin Williams, Bill Cosby and George Carlin – and downloaded them illegally from pirate websites, because there really was no other way of getting them in Pakistan. I listened to their sets over and over, analysing their structure and obsessing over their cadences. Through repeat listening, I learned the importance of a setup, the power of a callback and the many ways in which you can embolden the punch line. I imagined scenarios in which hecklers would appear and what cleverly acerbic one-liner I would use to shut them down. I studied the power of a simple observation and how the more specific to your own life you get, the more likely you are to speak to a larger shared experience. The great wisdom of stand-up comedy is that, if it happened to you, no matter what it is, then it probably happened to other people too.

For six months, I wrote, rewrote and then re-rewrote my set. I harvested experiences and observations from my life and mined them for deeper meanings. Watching cartoons on PTV as a child and being frustrated by how they were always cut off by the news. Shopping for clothes in preparation for the Eid festival. Attending bad dance parties. Uncles who believed in every conspiracy theory. Getting married. Airport security.

In retrospect, many of these topics are what most comedians consider 'hack' – a clichéd subject that has already been done too many times by too many comedians to have any potency left. In my defence, I didn't know that at the time. I had never been to a live stand-up comedy show and the four or five major comedians I listened to didn't cover those subjects. I actually thought I was breaking new ground when I joked about how bad airplane food was.

Once I felt the show was ready, with the material memorised and the delivery rehearsed, I booked an auditorium and advertised it through posters I designed and printed myself. On the night, Ishma sold tickets at the door while a friend served as usher. Then I got up and did the entire hour in front of a sceptical crowd.

There is a lot you figure out about stand-up comedy when you work without a safety net. You learn everything you need to know about delivery within the first ten minutes. You learn that, in Pakistan, audiences will give you a thirty-second grace period – so don't blow it. And you learn that sometimes trusting your instincts works. I got a standing ovation that night. Just like that, I was a Stand-up Comedian.

There was one strange speed bump I discovered that night, although it didn't really manifest until a day or so later. There is only one real taboo in Pakistan – religion. It turns out that when Pakistanis hear religion mentioned in the context of humour, they don't bother listening to what is being said; they just rush to be offended. I hadn't even considered what I said to be particularly blasphemous.

In my set, I had ridiculed the customs around Bakra Eid, a Muslim festival celebrated by sacrificing a goat (or a sheep, camel or cow). To outside observers, it would probably seem strange and barbaric; on Bakra Eid, the city roads are usually littered with animal innards and entire neighbourhoods smell of freshly cut meat. But there is a reason for it. The meat is then distributed among the poor. Think of it as if Santa Claus, instead of distributing presents, killed the reindeer then cut them up into small parcels and gave those to poor kids so they would have something to eat.

On stage, I shared the story of how I first discovered the origins of this tradition. How it honours the Prophet Abraham's willingness to sacrifice his son at God's command and how, at the last moment, God switched the frightened eldest son with a sheep. The first time I heard that tale, I was utterly horrified. 'So that means,' I said to my mother, 'if God hadn't switched the son, we'd be sacrificing the firstborn?' I then imitated the hysterical reaction of every male child emerging from the birth canal, demanding to know whether or not he was the first.

You had to be there.

The next day, a television presenter who'd been in the audience described my performance on his show and declared me blasphemous. In Pakistan that's a fatal crime. Friends who'd seen the show called me up to tell me I needed to go into hiding. For a few days I considered it, paranoid that every motorcycle driving past me was carrying a zealot with a machine gun. Many people have been killed with far less credible claims of blasphemy levelled against them. In the end, however, nothing came of it. The television presenter, thankfully, didn't have enough viewers for his message to reach anyone dangerous.

My own reaction to what had almost happened was to become strangely angry. I believed in my right to say what I wanted to, even if the rest of the country had no intention of honouring that right. Instead of dropping that bit, I kept it in my set. A year later, several university students threatened to beat me after a show, and some time after that a man snatched the microphone from my hand in the middle of a set and told me it was time I stopped talking. When I did finally stop doing that bit, though, it was only because I had worked up enough material not to need it anymore.

In retrospect, I realise how stupid it was of me. I could have been killed over a poorly crafted joke that only sometimes got a laugh. Luckily, the hyper-vigilant hysteria that now marks Pakistani religious discourse had not yet fully developed then and I was far enough below the radar of conventional media that no one noticed.

The bigger problem, I discovered, was that after an encore performance the next week, I ran out of audiences in Karachi. There just weren't enough people aware of or interested in stand-up comedy to justify the cost of renting an auditorium. I took the show to Lahore and Islamabad, where two nights in each city exhausted their supply of crowds as well. I had spent almost a full year working on an hour of stand-up material and, even though it was successful each time I performed it, there was no one left to perform it for.

With Black Fish's demise, there was a shortage of entertainment options for event managers trying to find ways of making corporate events more entertaining than just fifty suits swapping business cards. I snagged a few of those gigs and regretted each one. When I performed to an audience in an auditorium, they all sat facing me and had me as their only point of shared interest for the duration of the show. In corporate shows, you look out over a series of round tables, around which are seated bored businessmen, who have been forced by their paymasters to be there and who only want the food to be served so they can go home. Every corporate show ended in sweat and shattered self-esteem.

Today, though, I understand how important those terrible shows were for me. I had been fortunate enough that the novelty value of my public performances ensured each one successful. In that first year, people were just impressed by the sheer balls of this skinny kid standing on stage for an hour, and they applauded and laughed. But at corporate shows, I had to work hard for each laugh and earn every response. A comedian always learns more about the craft when doing badly. That's why the good shows all blur into one vague memory of people clapping, while each bad show is an individual shard of high-definition sharpness.

--------- • ---------

A year after my first show, Ishma left for Melbourne to get her master's degree in psychology. We had been married a full year at that point and been together for three, so her departure left me feeling suddenly alone. Those were the waning days of my first foray into advertising; shortly afterwards I jumped to Dawn News. With no one to spend time with when I got home from work, I poured all my time into stand-up, writing new material as fast as I could and then touring it through the major cities of Pakistan when my schedule allowed. More than one person pointed out how much of my stand-up became about watching porn and masturbating. You write about what you know, I guess.

Ishma finished her degree in a year and came home, by which time I was too busy with the channel to do much more comedy. I didn't do another new show until a week after walking away from the burning wreckage of Benazir Bhutto's bus. In between, my career as a stand-up comedian had started to evaporate. The launch of the channel and subsequent barrage of breaking news left me with barely any free time to spend with my wife and parents, and the work involved in producing a stand-up show was too demanding to achieve much in the little time available to me. However, I couldn't stop thinking like a comedian. Once you train your brain to focus on stray observations and then mine them for comedic potential, it's difficult to stop. Comedians are a lot like writers in that regard. A writer's presence of mind is always bisected; one half is engaged in whatever life events are unfolding in front of him and the other half is watching from a distance, trying to decide if there is anything there worth cataloguing for literary use. I found myself doing much the same all the time, except that instead of trying to weigh the emotional worth of a moment and hoping to discover some human truth in it, I was always trying to discover how it could be spun into a metaphor for the perfect dick joke.

Standing in front of the smoking husk of Benazir Bhutto's convoy and trying to keep from stepping in human remains, my brain threw up the only defensive shield it could find – it forced me to think of comedy. If the world was going to be so twisted and ugly and full of brutality that just living in it was becoming unbearable, I needed to find a way to make my own existence more tolerable and to come to terms with such horrific confrontations with reality. After I walked home and slept long enough to bury everything I had just seen under layers of repressing concrete, I woke up with a desperate need to do comedy. I booked the auditorium for a show to be held five days later and then stayed up all night writing.

Every idea that I had been storing, without realising I was doing so, was unpacked and stretched out. It was the first time I had considered comedy as a way of channelling my anger and, as a result, I think this was when I truly found my voice as a comedian. The first show had been a pastiche of impressions – harmless observations about Pakistani life filtered through Seinfeld-esque comedy structures. Those structures didn't work anymore. I couldn't exactly get up on stage and say, 'So what's the deal with suicide bombers? Doesn't it suck when they kill everyone you know and love and leave you a shattered, shivering wreck with no hope for the future? What's up with that?'

On the day of the show, I was worried that no one would come. The city had just suffered physical and existential trauma on a massive scale and people might find my attempt to do comedy so soon afterwards offensive at the very least. But I needn't have worried. Karachiites have a resilience that can be almost shocking. A bomb blast in the morning doesn't affect the evening's plans. From a distance this can look callous in the extreme, but that is an unfair characterisation. Karachi doesn't give up because Karachi can't afford to give up. Giving up once means you might as well surrender in perpetuity.

In the end, 300 people turned up at that show and I still consider my performance that evening the most honest I have ever done. For one hour, I constructed jokes about the strangeness we were all experiencing, and for one hour the audience reacted with the most desperate laughter I have ever heard. Each laugh was an exultant bark tinged with relief.

After the show, however, I was confronted with the same problem I had had after my first show. I could do it a couple more times in Karachi, maybe a few shows in Lahore and Islamabad, and then an entire hour of new material would be consigned to corporate events (where most of it would have to be edited for adult language and content, because apparently people working in offices have the sensibilities of prudish Victorians).

I had started to expand the list of comedians I was listening to around that time. From Seinfeld, Cosby and Chris Rock, I had graduated to Patton Oswalt, Louis CK, Jimmy Pardo and Bill Burr – all of them American comedians who were pushing the boundaries of stand-up comedy with stylistic inventions and thematic confidence. (There are no British comedians on this list. I tried but I couldn't understand any of the cultural references made by Brit comics. American culture's ubiquity makes the comedic references more relatable.) I studied their ability to inject their personal lives into their acts and use comedy to define their individual points of view.

The other major revelation in my understanding of stand-up comedy was podcasts. While fiddling around with my new iPod, I accidentally discovered comedy podcasts, just when comedians discovered they could make comedy podcasts. My weekly addiction became a show called *Never Not Funny*, recorded by LA comic Jimmy Pardo with a rotating panel of comedian friends. They would talk about their lives as comics, sharing stories about driving several hours for small gigs, performing in shitty comedy clubs in middle America and mastering their craft by doing hundreds of shows a year. Lacking a stand-up comedy fraternity of my own, I lived vicariously through them, injecting myself into their experiences. I know – it sounds quite pathetic.

Once, out of desperation, I emailed Patton Oswalt. It was a long tortured cry for help, asking for any advice he might have in my quest to become a better comedian, and the whole thing probably read as a creepy Anne-Wilkes-from-*Misery* attempt to ingratiate myself. To my surprise, he replied a day later with advice that genuinely changed my stand-up comedy career:

> I'm going to tell you what I tell every aspiring comedian who emails me. GO ON STAGE A LOT. DO NOT ASK ANYONE HOW TO DO YOUR MATERIAL. YOU MUST DEVELOP AT YOUR OWN, UNIQUE PACE. Advice at this stage of your career is useless. You're on the right track and don't even know it. Just keep going on stage, and writing, and loving what you do. I know it sounds like a douche-y cliché, but if you focus on being really, really good, everything else will fall right into place. You watch. Good luck. Don't quit.

I only recently realised that what he sent me was probably a form reply, something he could copy and paste and send to the thousands of amateur comedians who must email him for advice all the time. It didn't matter, though, as I took his wisdom to heart.

The first of the open-mic nights began popping up in Karachi at that time, one every few months. I became a regular fixture, trying new material at each one. The goal I set for myself was a new hour of comedy every year. I thought that was fairly reasonable and the only way to guarantee that audiences would return. Again, I would only later discover that most comedians spend several years honing a single hour of material and my goals were borderline suicidal. To hell with bliss, ignorance breeds creativity.

Still, those bimonthly open-mics and a few neutered corporate gigs weren't enough. I needed to find regular weekly performance venues and audiences willing to watch me struggle my way through new setups. And then I discovered Second Life.

12

Second Life is an online virtual world where you can be anything and do anything. It's like the Matrix, except it turns out Neo was less likely to wear black leather and carry guns and more likely to dress like a large human-kitten hybrid and engage in virtual sex with a Victorian robot using inflatable genitalia.

You log in and interact with a fully rendered, three-dimensional world in which people can create whatever they want and often do. Your presence there is represented by an avatar that you can customise down to the tiniest hair. Of course, you're still sitting in front of a computer using a mouse and keyboard, but it feels like virtual reality sometimes. Or, rather, 'felt'. Second Life, like most things on the internet, had a remarkable flowering, a time when it was poised to take over the world and CHANGE THE WAY WE LIVE. Then people got bored and moved on to Facebook. It's the internet. Even cat pictures will eventually be forgotten. Now Second Life is a barren landscape, populated with only a handful of truly dedicated patrons and people who still find it a convenient way of conducting illicit online affairs.

I mostly logged in to Second Life out of curiosity. Having read a few articles about junkyard apocalypse landscapes running into Star

Trek Enterprise simulations and Lovecraftian monsters, I downloaded the software and decided to poke around.

The first time I logged in, I appeared right next to two avatars having vigorous sex. A pixelated man with bulging biceps and the most lovingly rendered penis in existence was thrusting robotically into a pixelated woman with gargantuan breasts and a blurry vagina. As the fornicating animations spasmed, the two people controlling the avatars were typing descriptions of their imagined sex into the chat window.

> PumpingIron is giving you every inch, baby.
> Bigtittybooboofuck loves it.
> PumpingIron is spanking your ass.
>
> . . .
>
> PumpingIron is spanking your ass.
>
> . . .
>
> Where are you, Bigtittybooboofuck?
> Sorry, phone call . . . Yes, yes, spank me harder.

After several minutes of watching them achieve virtual climax, I began exploring the world with my generic male avatar. Soon I found a Steampunk city, abutting a nightclub built inside the skull of a shattered mega-robot. Large spiders walked past me; a pair of superheroes blazed overhead, holding hands as they twirled in the sky; and I was attacked by a half-dog, half-human samurai. How could I not go back?

Before long, my avatar was roaming Second Life, decked out as either a humanoid chimpanzee in a suit with a katana blade, or a gentleman automaton in a leather kimono. Also with a katana blade. After a few days of admiring virtual sculpture and watching strange beasties have sex, I stumbled across a comedy club.

Managed by a stand-up comedian sitting in Vancouver, Canada, the club hosted shows several times a week, with an audience of fifty or so avatars watching virtual comedians perform on an imaginary stage. The comedians would use microphones to transmit their voices into Second Life and the audience would show their appreciation by typing 'Hahaha' and 'LOL' in the group chat window.

I approached the club manager, a man with a mermaid's tail, and asked for a spot. For the next year, I logged in twice a week and performed stand-up comedy in Second Life.

Even here there were challenges to staging a successful performance. The biggest hindrance was Karachi's frequent unannounced power outages. I could be midway through a setup and I'd be disconnected from the internet because the electricity cut out. To pre-empt this, I issued a warning before each show that if I disappeared, it was either because there was no electricity or because a drone strike had targeted me.

The other problem was that most of the patrons at the virtual clubs were people logging in from America and UK on a weekday night. Time differences being what they were, this meant I had to do my shows at 3.30 am in Pakistan.

Fortunately, I had begun working on the breakfast show at Dawn News at this point and it meant waking up just half an hour before I normally would. So at 3.30 am, while it was still dark outside and my wife was fast asleep in the bedroom, I would sit on the lounge in my pyjamas, a handheld microphone plugged in to my laptop, and do stand-up comedy. At any point I would be performing to a virtual menagerie of creatures, from spindly robots to rainbow-coloured phoenixes. When a joke succeeded, the audience would react by typing their approval and when it failed they would type that out too.

At the end of the show, the club would pay me in virtual money that I would spend on renting an apartment in the Steampunk district. Then I'd log off and go to work at the news channel. I'm sure comedians have done stranger things to hone their craft, but I haven't heard of it.

I did have one experiment with Second Life sex, although that was my wife's fault. Ishma has always been hugely amused by my inability to flirt. The problem is that I can create the entire conversation in my head before the opening flirtation but, in the scenarios I foresee, it never ends well. To begin with, what will the opening salvo be? Everything sounds clichéd and ridiculous. When you're good-looking, it doesn't matter what you say because no one is listening. Girls are too busy admiring the depths of your eyes and your chiselled jaw. Meanwhile, I need to make sure the first thing I say is interesting, non-threatening, capable of creating a larger conversation and also with enough hint of attraction in it that I didn't end up as a bloody friend. There is no sentence in the English language capable of achieving all of that.

I had hoped this problem would become redundant once I got married, but Ishma was perpetually concocting scenarios in which she died tragically and I, after a period of grief, needed to find someone else.

'What'll you do?' she would ask. 'You can't hit on women to save your life. You'll end up dying alone.'

'Not at all. I'll just wait until someone desperate enough comes along and hits on me instead,' I'd reply, and then I'd get beaten over the head with a rolled-up *Cosmo*.

When I showed her Second Life, her immediate reaction was, 'You should totally use that to practise flirting!'

'Isn't that cheating?' I asked.

'Not if I say you can do it. Plus, it's online, so it's not real.'

I could have shown her news articles about marriages torn apart by virtual dalliances, but decided not to.

So one day, with Ishma helpfully interjecting, I gave it a try. The first thing I needed to do was make my avatar more sexually appealing. I could, with little effort, find someone willing to do the digital dirty with a humanoid chimp or a Victorian robot, but this was going to be a scientific experiment in flirtation, and so it needed as much versimilitude as possible. So I morphed into a handsome human male, with short blond hair, steel-grey eyes, a well-defined six-pack and arms like hydraulic machinery. That avatar was probably further away from my real physique than the chimp and robot. Then, dressed in a white shirt and pinstriped pants with a waistcoat, I went on the prowl. I teleported into several of Second Life's most popular clubs, but found them all a bit too BDSM-themed for my liking. The increasing prevalence of bondage culture in pornography has always disconcerted me. No one makes simple porn anymore – just two people having sex. Now everything is kinky. Whips and chains and ball gags and spankings have become the norm. It doesn't matter what your kink is, no matter how deep and dark and disturbing your fetish, someone has already filmed it and it probably has a whole slew of websites dedicated to it. Not that I'm a prude. I understand the importance of kinky sex; it makes the everyday, normal, boring sex more exciting. But if we film everything kinky, eventually we'll reach a place where we run out of kink. The last kinky porno ever made will be a pre-op transsexual midget in latex, having sex with a quadriplegic puppy that's dead at the time. Then it'll finish. Society will have run out of kink. But that isn't a good thing. If kinky sex becomes so prevalent that it is boring, then we'll need something new to replace it. Everyday boring sex will have to become the new kink. There will be websites dedicated to handholding, caressing a cheek, brushing away someone's hair. While at home, everyone will be having the kinkiest, most disturbing sex possible. There'll be whips and chains and spank paddles and gas masks.

Then, one day, your partner will turn to you and say, 'What's the kinkiest thing you've ever wanted to do?' And you'll know you shouldn't tell, but you're feeling vulnerable and open, because you spent the last hour suspended from the ceiling in chains and there are waffle-iron burns across your buttocks and the midget is crying in the corner. So you blush and you run your fingers through your hair. Maybe your ears grow a little warm. And you turn to your partner and say, 'The kinkiest thing I've ever wanted to do? Okay, I've never told anyone this before, but the kinkiest thing I've ever wanted to do is . . . cuddling.' And your partner calls you a pervert and throws you out.

Eventually I found a club vanilla enough not to have to promise a female avatar a strip of skin in exchange for conversation. After a while, it becomes easy to distinguish avatars owned by real women from those that are being controlled by sweaty men in their basements. The real women always give their avatars more realistic proportions – not breasts large enough to have moons orbiting them, just normal curves. Of course, there was still some risk that the owner would turn out to be a US senator in his underwear behind the pixels, but then that's always a possibility.

Choosing an attractive human female avatar with no extra appendages, I walked up and complimented her on her tattoo (Ishma, sitting beside me, suggested this would work as a nice icebreaker). The avatar thanked me for the compliment and so I asked her how she liked the club. Soon we were in an actual conversation. After half an hour of witty repartee, she asked to see my rented virtual apartment, so we teleported over.

'She wants to have sex with you,' Ishma said.

'Maybe she's just curious about the apartment,' I suggested.

'It's an apartment. Why would she care? She wants to have sex. Do it!'

Putting some soft jazz on my virtual sound system, I offered my companion a virtual drink. Then we began to strip off our virtual clothes. Each garment was removed by right-clicking on it and clicking 'remove' for it to disappear. This was accompanied by a description of the absent action.

ME: *I pull off my shirt, tossing it aside.*

HER: *I unbutton my blouse, freeing my breasts.*

Eventually we stood naked in front of each other. I quickly and discreetly opened a new window in the browser and purchased a penis that didn't shoot fire, pour steam or have tentacles, then our avatars began bopping and grinding. The descriptions began flowing hot and heavy, with me using all my English major skills and everything I had ever read when sneaking a peek at my aunt's Mills & Boons as a child.

ME: *I slowly trace my fingers across the curve of your hip before thrusting forward with my throbbing manhood.*

HER: *Yeah – fuck me, cowboy.*

The entire thing became too unsatisfying. I was laying some grammar on her, using words carefully chosen to arouse. She kept coming back with, 'Yeah, fuck me, yeah!' So I decided to end it. Typing furiously, I described the conclusion:

ME: *My back arches as I cry out, climaxing inside you.*

HER: *AAAGGGGGGGHHHIIIIIOOOOOOOOOOOOLLLLLLLLLLAA*

It was either the world's first onomatopoeic orgasm, or she passed out and hit her head on the keyboard. Either way, I never tried again.

--------- • ---------

After several months of regular Second Life stand-up performances, I began to build a following in-world. More comedy clubs appeared; my favourites were one set inside a sunken submarine and another in a junkyard. The former required all its patrons to appear in the form of marine life, with an audience composed of sharks, mer-people and various homages to Poseidon. The latter looked like a gathering of extras from the *Mad Max* set.

I started writing new material regularly, trying it out on stage, finding the beats within it that made it work and then writing more. It was the closest I had come to experiencing stand-up comedy the way comedians in the rest of the world did. I enjoyed the freedom to reuse material again and again, a luxury not afforded me by my small but loyal audience in real life. But I also started to wonder about the disposability of what I wrote.

Ideally, a well-crafted joke, honed and perfected over repeat performances, should have an extensive shelf life. Many comedians perform the same act over and over for years before replacing their bits. But up till now, I had been forced to abandon each set shortly after I wrote it. Instead of taking a year to write new comedy and then living with it for one more year, I began to wonder whether I could write on a weekly basis and then abandon it after one performance. This idle thought in time became a way for me to practise my writing skills. And so *News Weakly* was born.

News Weakly is probably the only thing in the world that began in Second Life, then became a stage performance in real life, and finally ended up on national television. I first had the idea when I realised that the same disposability I was contemplating for my comedy was something practised every day in news. Unlike writers, journalists are allowed a minimal amount of time to craft stories, publishing them and then instantly moving on to the next one. Those stories are consumed and then, if you work in print, forgotten by the next day or, if you are in television, by the next hour. It occurred to me that I could use the news as a basis for my comedy, at least for the purposes of this exercise.

At work I was still harvesting news stories for Dawn's breakfast show, so I would pick the top international news pieces and then write jokes around them. Then, in-world, I would perform them to the avatars in attendance. A week later, regardless of how proud I was of a bit, it was no longer relevant and I was forced to write something new.

I did this for a couple of months, and the popularity of the show grew each week. Then, in a burst of confidence, I decided to try taking it into the real world. I booked an auditorium for three weekends in a row and advertised the show as being new each week. The same audience could attend each show, I promised, and find it different from the last. To take some of the pressure off having to write an entire hour, I incorporated a projector so I could supplement my (admittedly) weaker jokes with garishly Photoshopped pictures. If it was a bit about the Chief Justice of Pakistan fixing his lazy eye on Musharraf, like a cyclopean beast, I presented it with a picture of him flash-frying the dictator with an eye-laser.

Even though the shows had full attendance, they weren't consistently funny. I had overreached myself by attempting a full hour each time. Still, the audiences were charitable and I was excited. *News Weakly* had survived being transferred into reality.

Around that time, I decided to leave the news department of Dawn News entirely. Azhar Abbas had just resigned, and the search for his successor had rendered the newsroom rife with political intrigue.

People who had spent the last two years together began knifing one another in the back in a manner that would have made the author of *Game of Thrones* proud. Having no appetite for office politics, I transferred to the features department. Features focuses on creating programming that can be put on air while the news team takes a cigarette break. There were debate shows, historical and social analysis shows, mini-documentaries and a new film review show. A producer cast me in the film review show *Cutting It*, in which a female co-host and I dissected the latest movies. Since Pakistan didn't yet have cinemas that showed anything released since the previous decade, all our reviews were based on bootleg copies.

Discovering that I could be put on screen without frightening away too many viewers, the management at Dawn News asked me if I would like to do a news satire show. Some of the other channels had their own such shows and they were among the most popular programming being put out at the time. As the tragedies that marked the daily news cycle of Pakistan developed a mundane regularity, I think Pakistanis began craving the more cheerful surprises that allowed laughter. Comedy and horror rely on the same element of surprise, but to radically different effect.

Just wrapping up my latest attempt at bringing *News Weakly* to the stage, I agreed to try turning it into a TV show. The only caveat from the channel was that there was absolutely no budget, so I had to do it alone. The absence of a budget wasn't surprising to me, or indeed to anyone at the channel by then. Dawn News had begun with a promise of mature and responsible journalism, to contrast the hysteria put out by the rest. In that goal, it was successful and viewers frequently appreciated it for that. But then those viewers switched over to the other channels, to watch politicians hurl abuse at each other and gawp at footage of severed heads. The channel was, as a result, respected but haemorrhaging money. All the CEOs in Pakistan watched it, but none of them felt it was worth spending their advertising money on it. So production budgets shrank and salaries were discreetly trimmed.

Even then, to Dawn News's credit, it attempted to cling to its vision. The channel provided measured reportage of Benazir Bhutto's death and of her husband, Asif Ali Zardari – the most corrupt man in Pakistan's corruption-filled history – riding a wave of sympathy all the way to the presidency. Suicide bombings became a daily event and crime was so common no one was left unaffected by it. At least I wouldn't have to worry about a lack of content.

13

For twenty-eight weeks, I wrote, produced, directed, edited and hosted a news satire show on national television in Pakistan. It was the happiest I've ever been professionally. I'd like to blame the fact that I was doing everything myself on the absence of a budget, but the truth is it was the only way I would have done it. The descriptor 'control freak' can be bandied about, but for me *News Weakly* was a labour of love.

I realised early on that every aspect of producing a comedy show has an influence on the comedy itself, from the way it's lit to the way it's edited. And I knew I had a very specific comedic sensibility I wanted to get across to the viewer. For the show to succeed, it needed to combine dry wit with broad slapstick, and I had to learn to do it all myself. My stand-up was always acerbic so, to counter the morbid tone of the news I'd be covering, I needed the show to have a more ridiculous feel to it, while still keeping it informative. It was, in the end, airing on a news channel and pies thrown at my face, while funny to me, might hurt the Dawn News brand. I needed to ensure it had the right tone and I think it took me the first few episodes to sort that out.

Every weekday, I would go to work with a pair of one-terabyte external hard disks. Plugging them into the office network, I'd then trawl for anything worth saving. This meant going through the major stories being captured off the Reuters and Associated Press feeds, as well as watching all the local press conferences and bulletin stories. Anything that seemed to have a nugget of controversy or hypocrisy would go onto the hard disks, which meant they were mostly full by the end of the week. Once the footage was harvested, I went home and took quick notes on everything, cataloguing it by subject and nationality and then time-coding anything worth returning to. Late on Friday, the work would start. At 9 pm, late enough to have allowed for a full week of stories to develop, I'd sit down in my pyjamas at a desk at home, drain a can of Red Bull, smoke half a pack of cigarettes, and write. The script for each episode took up to ten hours of continuous writing, rewriting and re-rewriting. In those hours I was lost to the world – every iota of concentration was focused on structuring jokes correctly. If a bomb had gone off right behind me, I'd have made sure I hit 'save' on the document first, then I'd have unplugged the laptop and tucked it under my shirt before considering evacuation.

Karachi mornings are signalled first by the Fajr call to prayer, mournfully echoing outwards from neighbourhood mosques, and then by the lilting coos of Koel birds as they greet the sunrise. I let them serve as my alarm clock, reminding me that I also needed sleep to continue functioning. I'd then save the script to multiple places on my computer and the internet, and email a copy to a senior editor at *Dawn* newspaper, who had been tasked with checking it for anything that might get me killed or the channel attacked. The latter was the bigger concern, because the channel's equipment cost significantly more than one comedian. I had spent enough time in news to know the major taboos – avoid discussions of Islam and try not to say anything about one particular political party in Karachi, who tended to respond to criticisms with targeted gunshots.

Then I'd pass out. I would sleep until noon, before waking, showering and shaving and leaving for Dawn News. I always booked one of the studios for two hours every Saturday afternoon and, by the time I was suited and plastered with makeup, it would be dressed with the custom-built set for my show. The goal was to make *News Weakly* seem, at first glance, like a credible news show, with the comedic content only becoming evident once you unmuted the sound.

The set, designed superbly by the Dawn News creative department, looked like an authentic news studio. It featured an illuminated backdrop with a map of the world stretched across it, plus a burnished steel desk, the whole thing lit so brilliantly you could fry an egg where I sat. In an ideal world, we'd have had a budget for a live audience so I wasn't reading the script out to four distracted cameramen and a sound technician; but those were luxuries the channel could no longer afford. Over the next two hours I directed myself, doing multiple takes of each segment of the show. Every episode was twenty-two minutes of airtime long, with an interview slotted into the final seven minutes. My guest interviewees alternated between the editorial talent within Dawn News and outside writers and academics. The goal was to balance the earlier fifteen minutes of farce with something more substantial than my face.

Once it was all recorded, I took the footage home on the same terabyte disks for editing. The rest of the weekend was spent apologising to my then-pregnant wife for neglecting her. Sunday night I'd boot up the hard disks, open video-editing software and begin finessing the show.

There are tricks you learn while editing comedy that accentuate the punch lines. They only make sense to video editors and comedians;

to acquire them I obsessively watched episodes of *The Daily Show with Jon Stewart* and *The Colbert Report*. Both aired on Comedy Central in the US, where I'd watched them during college, but in Pakistan I had to download them illegally. In my defence, all this piracy was for a higher purpose. I learned when to run a close-up, that a hard jump-cut is always funnier than a soft dissolve and that sometimes you let the show sit in silence, stretching out the awkward pauses for effect. I'd edit until the Koels cooed again and, after a quick nap, drop off the footage to the office for its Monday-night airing.

The first five or six episodes were terrible. I have enough distance from them now to know that. But I can also watch them and see the exact moments when I started getting better and learned how to perform comedy to a camera. I'll never have the camera presence of a Stephen Colbert or Moin Akhter, and my face looks distractingly crooked on camera for some reason, but I still developed enough control over the timing and delivery to make comedy work on screen.

By the time the show had run its course, I'd covered the final days of the Bush presidency, the election of Barack Obama, the terrorist attack on the Sri Lankan cricket team in Lahore and the big terrorist attack in Mumbai. There were no slow news weeks; Pakistan, and the rest of the world too, reliably provided enough fodder for satire, even though sometimes I had to work hard to find comedy in the tragedy. (Sometimes, though, I didn't have to work hard at all, like when a shoe was thrown at President Bush, which led to a shoe-flinging epidemic around the world.)

There were some phenomena I discovered that could be guaranteed to write their own punch lines. The most reliable was that, no matter who the politician was and where in the world they were speaking, if they espoused an opinion on something, you could find – with enough research – earlier footage of them saying the exact opposite with just as much conviction. I also realised, more than ever before, that every news story is merely a repeat of events that had occurred previously, with minor changes in the cast of characters at best.

I wrote, performed and filmed a complete rap song, with a classic 1980s-style music video; I even performed a Pakistani version of a Billy Joel classic. I was deliriously happy. For the first time in my life, comedy wasn't something I did on the side: it was my only job – which is why I was heartbroken when it didn't last.

News Weakly wasn't a success by the channel's standards. Of course, by then the channel wasn't a success by its own standards. There just weren't enough viewers tuning into Dawn News anymore. Azhar Abbas's departure and the ensuing editorial confusion was reflected in the on-screen news coverage. To distract from that, the channel began airing more extraneous content; but they did not appreciate that when a bomb goes off in a Pakistani city and kills several hundred people, viewers want updates on the attack and don't want to watch a cooking show instead.

News Weakly was barely advertised or promoted, and halfway through its run its timeslot was abruptly changed. Finally, the owner of the channel watched an episode and deemed it not to her liking. After seven months, it was pulled off the air.

If it sounds like I am defensive about the quality of the show, then of course I bloody am. I worked harder on that than anything I have ever done since. I acknowledge its weaknesses, especially in the first few episodes, but it became something worthwhile by the end. To this day, when in Pakistan, I am approached by people who saw it and loved it. I wish I could have done more, but I suppose I am also grateful for the chance to do as many episodes as I did.

On the very day the channel owners informed me that the show was being cancelled and the next episode would be my last, *News*

Weakly was mentioned in an article on news satire shows in the *Guardian* and praised on the Comedy Central website. I had poured everything I knew about comedy and television production into the show and people liked it. But sometimes that isn't enough.

14

When *News Weakly* was given the axe, I decided it was time to make my exit from Dawn News. The channel became confused about what it wanted to be and that confusion was becoming evident on screen. Confronted with rapidly plummeting viewership numbers, it responded by aping its competition, adding a layer of salacity to every news story that marked a distinct departure from its original stated goals. Budgets continued to be cut and soon an employee cull was initiated that drastically reduced staffing levels. Not keen on returning to the news department, given its redefined approach to journalism, and having the one show I thought was the best contribution I could create for the channel taken off air, I figured it wasn't long before I too would be sent packing.

So, in 2009, a month after my daughter was born, I quit. The decision was made easier by the management halving all of our salaries, something I couldn't afford with the added cost of diapers and paediatric visits. With deep regret and a fairly sizeable helping of crow, I reached out to friends in advertising and returned to the industry.

For the next three years, I worked as a creative director at JWT. Essentially, I was doing exactly the same thing I had done when I was a junior art director, except with a larger salary and even longer hours.

Being a new father staved off much of the inevitable soul crushing that advertising inculcates. The combination of sleep-deprived delirium and overwhelming love for my daughter, Anya, made it all a great deal more tolerable.

I also managed to return to stand-up, working up a new hour of material while singing Anya to sleep in the lost hours of the night. Drawing on national politics and combining that with the insights gained from washing poo off a baby's bottom, I was able to take a more personal view of the world onto the stage. It was no longer enough for me to make fun of the way the world was – I found that my comedy became about how I interacted with the world. There were also increasing amounts of anger in my material, born of my frustration that the entire planet wasn't working hard enough to make itself a better place for my daughter.

I like to think I had now embraced a selfless desire for social change, filtered through a comedic sensibility, but really it was probably just a mutated form of narcissism. Up till then, in every conversation I had I'd been thinking silently, 'Talk about me! Why aren't you talking about me?!' But that had changed now; my universe had a new centre. These days, I just wanted to talk about my baby all the time. Now I was demanding: 'Talk about this extension of me!'

The disappointment of losing *News Weakly* and leaving Dawn News was counterbalanced by the exposure the show had given me. During its run, it was noticed by a major international comedy website, and I was asked to write about my experiences as a Pakistani stand-up comedian. The two-part article I wrote was quoted on Comedy Central's blog, which led to me being contacted by a comedy promoter/producer in Australia. I received an email from John Pinder, who I later learned is a bit of a legend in Australian comedy, inviting me to be part of a new comedy festival he was organising in Sydney.

Intrigued by my article, he asked if I had enough material to perform a full hour. He probably thought I was being arrogant when I replied I had enough for three, but he let the invitation stand.

It was called the World's Funniest Island Festival and was going to be held on Cockatoo Island in Sydney Harbour over three days. It boasted an international roster of comedians, of whom I was undoubtedly the least famous and successful. Still, it was the first evidence I had ever received that I was considered an actual stand-up comedian by someone other than myself. International appraisal is important when your art has no local context against which to judge yourself. I instantly had visions of being noticed by comedy agents and promoters at the festival and achieving international stardom. First step, a small island in Sydney, then the world. Except my visa never arrived.

I should have known there would be trouble when the festival organisers didn't respond to my suggestion that they should arrange a performance visa for me six months before the festival. 'We'll do it in the last few weeks,' one of the contacts reassured me. 'Don't worry – I've arranged visas for musicians with criminal records as long as my arm. You won't be a problem.'

'I will,' I wrote back. 'None of those musicians were Pakistanis.'

The thing to understand is that the Pakistani passport isn't so much a passport as it is a voucher for free rectal exams, redeemable in airports around the world. Sure enough, hours before my flight to Sydney was due to leave, John finally called me up to say he was deeply sorry but the embassy couldn't get my visa processed in time.

There are few things as depressing as unpacking your suitcases a couple of hours after you packed them, without having gone anywhere. Two nights of shows had been advertised on the festival website and program, and I had been told I'd be doing a promotional appearance on Australian TV, on *Good News Week*. Instead, I stayed in Karachi, and all my dreams and aspirations dissipated like cigarette smoke.

I never found out why I wasn't allowed into Australia for the festival. Perhaps the Australian embassy considered me too much of a security risk. I'm not sure what their concerns might have been. Did they think I was raised in the comedy caves of Jalalabad, where I was taught classic Al-Qaeda comedy?

I like to think I handled the disappointment well, overcoming it with good grace and forced positivity. But Ishma says I was quite unbearable for several weeks after, moping and sniping bitterly at anyone in biting distance. Eventually, though, I managed to get over how devastatingly unfair the universe was and refocus on just doing more stand-up comedy right where I was. I got back on stage every chance I got, even turning the entire Australian-invitation-then-rejection experience into ten minutes of stand-up.

By this point I had fallen into a pattern of working on a new show annually and then touring it across the country, with corporate gigs interspersed in between. Second Life was no longer a viable stage, with power outages increasing in the city as the Zardari government gulped down every possible resource that could be monetised. Violence became routine, and almost every show I did in those years had to be delayed or rescheduled because of a suicide attack elsewhere in the city or a city-wide shutdown caused by political parties on a rampage. Still, I kept doing shows and people kept coming, all of us desperate to escape the reality pressing in on us.

I found a new way to express my frustrations when, in 2010, I was invited to write a weekly column for a new local paper. *Express Tribune*, an English-language daily, was affiliated with the *International Herald Tribune*. I had been brought to the attention of the editors by one of the ex-Dawn News people now working at the new paper, and so I met with Omar Quraishi, an old hand at editing opinion columns, who wanted something different from the stodgy traditionalists who wrote for his competitors. Missing the practice that writing comedy on a weekly schedule provides, I agreed.

I wrote those columns every week for over two years, finally stopping when I left Pakistan for Australia. They were due every Tuesday night for Thursday publication, so once a week I would guzzle a Red Bull and bleed out 600 words. Surprisingly, what I had thought would be a short and unnoticed experiment resulted in me becoming more widely known as a comedian in Pakistan than all my stand-up comedy and TV work combined. During the writing of those eighty-eight individual columns, I saw attendance at my shows increase dramatically; I achieved a miniscule amount of celebrity and received enough death threats to make me confront my mortality every time I left the house. Wounded by satire, politicians threatened to beat me; a TV host who had delighted in publicly berating a gang-rape victim tried to sue me; even Pakistan's intelligence agency sent me a warning.

I'm not sure why I didn't give in to the rational advice my own brain was giving me – that the columns weren't worth dying over. But I couldn't stop writing them. They came from a place of anger, strained through whatever comedic sensibilities I had developed over the years. Each one was a compulsion. Having brought my daughter into a shitty world, where the most terrible people routinely destroyed innocent lives, I felt like those columns were my attempt to improve things. Or at least to react with the only weapon I had.

I railed against Pakistan's horrendous blasphemy laws and the continued massacring of religious minorities. Of course, none of it made any difference. I was just a court jester trying to point out the emperor's nudity. In the end, the emperor was still the emperor and I was still a clown.

While my columns gave vent to my political and ideological frustrations, my stand-up comedy became more biographical. On stage, I'd spend an hour talking about diapers, about the fear that being a parent instils in you and about how much I hated working in advertising.

Even though I was getting better as a stand-up comedian – each show refined my stage presence and delivery – I was getting bored with the limited options available to me as a comedian. I couldn't travel to international venues or book shows in other countries; I was barely earning enough from the comedy to cover the costs of each show in my own country. So when I was contacted by the BBC about doing a show for an audience in London, I was ecstatic.

'If they pay for my ticket,' I told Ishma, 'then maybe we can cover the rest and make a trip out of it.'

I wrote back, telling them I'd be thrilled to be a part of whatever they had planned.

'Excellent,' they replied. 'Do you have a Skype connection?'

They were planning a show for the BBC Asian Network, giving some of Britain's top comedians of Indian and Pakistani decent stage time. Turned on to my comedy by a producer in London, who had discovered me through YouTube, they decided to include a genuine Pakistani comedian in the mix. The show was going to be performed to a live audience in the BBC Radio Theatre, with a celebrity host and each comedian getting ten minutes of stage time. I was the only one for whom that stage time would be virtual. To complicate matters further, my office sent me on a business trip to Thailand on the same day as the show.

We pulled it off; the success of the show was a testament to modern technology. Factoring in the time difference, I did my entire set at 1.30 am, in a hotel room in Bangkok. I borrowed a co-worker's laptop, adding it to mine, and paid off the hotel's IT manager so I could access their broadband connection. Then, with one laptop providing video footage over Skype and the other sending audio, I performed stand-up comedy to the audience in London. They could see and hear me through large screens on stage, whereas I could only hear their response with a one-second delay. This meant that every time I finished a bit, I had to assume there was laughter I needed to pause for before I started the next one. If that had failed, my backup plan had been to start stripping, just to stave off any awkwardness.

Since they could only see my head and shoulders, I did the entire show in a shirt, blazer and underwear, with the laptop's camera angled so as to block the view of the bed just behind me. Later, a reviewer marvelled at how I was able to overcome the technical difficulties and deliver a successful stand-up show. To be honest, though, after Second Life, this was hardly the strangest show I had ever done.

A few weeks after that, in February 2012, I was invited to perform at a TEDx event held in Islamabad. It ended up being my last stand-up comedy show in Pakistan, because in June, Ishma, Anya and I left for Australia.

I, AMERICA

15

Moving to Australia was the second time I left Pakistan. The first was when I went to America for college in 1998.

Even though I ended up returning home in 2002, when I boarded that flight to Virginia in August 1998, both my parents and I thought I was leaving for good. That was, after all, the traditional way; child goes to foreign land for education, gets job in same land after graduating and ends up settling there for the rest of his life. My mother's brother had done much the same decades earlier, living in New York since the seventies. America was where people from the developing world sent their children to have better lives.

It was something I had dreamed of for years before going there. Growing up in Karachi, I read American comics, watched American movies and listened to American music. By the time I was applying to American universities, I knew as much about America as I did about Pakistan. I wasn't alone in this either – the entire planet is bathed in American media. When I was finishing high school, friends who were leaving for British universities faced a more alien culture than those of us bound for the United States.

My own fascination with the 'land of the free and the home of the brave' began with Archie comics. I and everyone I knew collected thin digests packed with the adventures of the red-haired teenager and his friends as they lived out their eternal youth in Riverdale, the apotheosis of smalltown America. As a little boy, I dreamed of visiting Pop Tate's 'Chok'lit Shoppe' and ordering a soda, of riding around in a jalopy with Betty and Veronica, and running through the school halls under Mr Weatherbee's stern gaze. It didn't help that everyone told me I looked like Jughead and Dilton Doiley's illegitimate son.

Even the toys my friends and I collected were American (although they were probably made in Taiwan or China). We knew the name of every GI Joe action figure and could sing along to the theme song – a Pakistani children's chorus extolling the virtues of 'a real American hero'. By the time I entered my teens, I graduated to super-hero comics. Twenty-one pages of full-colour adventures starring an endless array of spandex-wrapped warriors. Epic sagas held together by a pair of staples.

I was thirteen when I read my first Marvel comic, winning it in a game of table tennis played against a boy at school. I can't remember his name anymore, nor what he looked like, nor indeed what collateral I offered against the comic if I lost. All I remember is that in a best-of-three match, my winning point was hard fought for. He was gracious in defeat, handing over without complaint the X-Men comic he had brought back from a holiday to America. I took it home, hid it from my mother ('Comics ruin your English,' she used to say) and only took it out once I was sure everyone was asleep.

Oh, to read that comic for the first time again. Mutant heroes with muscles of steel and eyes that exploded with power. Villains who could bend iron and control thoughts. Over the next few years I spent all my money on comics. Old second-hand issues purchased in Sunday bazaars were piled up on my bedroom floor. My mother complained and scolded. She hid them and I bought more. She tore them up and I had tantrums. Finally she let me be.

America had become for me the land where men clung to walls, flew through the sky, transformed into beasts and avenged their dead parents. America was the land of superheroes. And superheroes fought for what was right. I mourned the fact that there were no Pakistani superheroes. I tried imagining them myself, but found it impossible to come up with a believable origin. We had no Norse gods from which to descend, for example. We only had Allah – and for me to have him bestowing such powers on anyone other than the Prophet Muhammad was blasphemy, that much I knew. And a good superhero is not blasphemous.

Pakistan had no radioactivity, and no spiders with infectious bites. This was a time when the idea of our country having possession of a nuclear bomb was something that only a small military and intelligence elite considered a distinct reality. For me, it was just another frustrating dead end. And besides, what would the hero's motto be? Truth, Justice and the Pakistani Way? What was the Pakistani way? For the first time in my life, I became frustrated with being a Pakistani. Why was I born in a land without superheroes? I think when, five years later, I got off the plane in Washington DC, I still half expected to see Superman fly overhead.

Near the end of my A-levels, I gained admission to the University of Virginia's engineering department with the aim of studying computer science. A bout of jaundice the year before had left me bedridden long enough to learn how to code a website and convince me that my future lay in internet wizardry. But I should have known I wouldn't last as a computer science major, given that my entire reason for applying to UVa had nothing to do with the quality of its computer science department; I had read that Edgar Allan Poe, one of my favourite authors, had studied there and so had based my entire college selection criteria on that arbitrary nugget of information.

Still, a combination of decent SAT scores and enough teacher recommendations did the trick. A couple of months after mailing off my application, I received a thick envelope. Inside was a booklet extolling the university's many fine attributes as a place of higher learning, plus a guide for international students on how best to integrate into American society. It contained charming bits of information like 'Use deodorants as others may be sensitive to your smells' and 'Do not intrude on anyone's personal space'. Apparently, America believed the rest of the world went around pressing their noses and underarms up against one another. I would have been insulted had I not been so excited.

The challenge wasn't admission, though. Apply to enough colleges and someone or other is bound to accept you – it's why liberal arts colleges exist, after all. Nor was it finances, although the fact that the rupee had about the same value against the dollar as a fistful of mud didn't help. However, if you create enough of a sob story about growing up in an impoverished nation, with dreams of a better education than what is on offer locally, and if you sprinkle some promises about wanting to take the West's great values and training back to make a difference in your homeland, then someone will give you a scholarship or offer financial aid. No, the biggest challenge was the visa.

Pakistanis envy, at a level that can never be accurately conveyed, people with foreign passports. People who can travel to any country in the world and get a visa on arrival. People who can realistically consider travelling to any country in the world. These are experiences those of us cursed with the dark-green Pakistani passport can never enjoy.

Every student's future hung on the whim of a random visa officer at the US embassy. Using a mystic set of unknown criteria, he or she determined whether it was safe to let you into their country. We had all heard stories about students who had graduated the year before and applied to enter America or Britain, only to be rejected with no reason given. For those of us applying for foreign visas in the early months of 1998, however, there was an added problem: India was about to nuke us.

Actually, the Indian government nuked an unassuming stretch of desert in its own country. To my knowledge, the desert had done nothing to deserve this irradiation, and had in fact been behaving exactly as deserts always behave, but somehow that was enough to provoke the Indian government and they detonated a nuclear bomb underneath it. Yet, while that underground explosion was thousands of kilometres away from Pakistan, they might as well have created a mushroom cloud over Islamabad.

Pakistanis dropped whatever they were doing the moment the news broke and, after gawping wordlessly in the general direction of their hated neighbour, turned to their leaders and demanded that they do something about this before we all had to learn the Indian national anthem. Everyone wanted evidence that we could also wage war against innocent stretches of uninhabited land, and they wanted it right away. Everyone, that is, except the students at the tail end of their A-levels who had applied to colleges in the West and were now waiting to be granted visas for entry. We begged and pleaded, cried and cursed, praying that common sense would prevail and Pakistan would not take the nuclear bait. Our intended destinations mirrored our hopes, urging our government to keep its finger off the button.

But their pressure proved as useless as our fervent prayers and, less than a week later, Pakistan declared war on a local mountain range. Seismic sensors around the world registered the unmistakable signature of a nuclear test. The subsequent cries of a few thousand students with international aspirations were probably erroneously catalogued as aftershocks. Pakistani newspapers heralded the arrival of the 'Islamic Bomb', a name that was probably a mistake on the public relations front. Soon after, stories of rejected visas began to circulate.

I got my chance a few weeks later. A letter summoned me to the American embassy at Islamabad. I was to bring my passport and evidence of college admission. On the morning of the interview, I reached the embassy at exactly 7 am, having been told it was first-come first-serve. To get to the embassy, we had to pass through a quarter-mile of checkpoints and barriers. Guard dogs and armed men lined the way but, instead of the kind of focused alertness one would expect, they all just seemed bored and uninterested. This was before American embassies became the single focal point of every terrorist's fantasies.

The prospect of an American visa, being the kind of rare and respected artefact that it was, ensured that everyone was on their best behaviour, out of fear that they might hurt their already minuscule chances of getting one. Even terrorists had to get to America before they could commit any act of terrorism.

Despite being there two hours before the embassy officially opened, I was thirtieth in line. Families ahead of me looked as though they had slept the night on the concrete footpath. By the time the embassy opened for business at 9 am, the queue behind me wrapped around itself thrice, with several hundred hopefuls already feeling the flat slap of the Islamabad sun beating down on them. Old people had brought their younger family members with them, to hold their position in the slowly advancing queue while they took some time out. Little children who had started the day playfully jumping in and out of line were soon wailing with boredom. Everyone else just swatted flies and sweated.

It was another hour and a half before I finally made it inside and by then little social knots had begun to form in the line. People struck up conversations with those around them, turning the queue into a series of conversational clusters. The topics included: the standard cursing of India for forcing Pakistan's nuclear hand; how that might affect the chances of our getting a visa to America; how so-and-so's friend's cousin had been rejected recently with no reason given . . . and why won't anyone shut that damn kid up? (Although, poor thing, it really is quite hot.) Another few hours and I was fairly sure tribalism would start to emerge, with raiding parties and chieftains.

Thankfully, I didn't stay long enough to see that eventuate. I reached the front of the queue and entered the embassy, and found myself in a waiting room. The same thirty people who had been ahead of me in line were sprawled on chairs inside, waiting for their name to be called. By this time, the combination of exhaustion, heat stroke and anxiety had taken its toll on my psychological state; I suddenly became acutely aware of where I was. If my understanding of international law was sound, then I was standing on American soil. I had already entered America and was probably being watched by security cameras that fed footage of me to teams of CIA analysts hidden deep inside the bowels of this fortified complex, analysing my every move, every expression, every bead of sweat.

What would be the wrong move to make? What would single me out as a potential terrorist threat? If I slumped too casually in my chair, would that seem as though I was trying too hard not to look suspicious, and therefore render me more suspicious? Or if I sat upright and looked aware of my surroundings, would it seem as if I was hiding something?

I began to sweat. My underarms became slick and my forehead dripped. This would surely register on any heat-sensitive thermal-imaging cameras that were trained on me. It was over. Any moment now a team of marines would explode through the doorway, training lasers on and obliterating me before I had a chance to tell them how my appreciation for their popular culture (specifically the creative output of Marvel and DC) made me worthy of entering their nation and being a productive contributor to their intellectual economy.

When my name was called over the loudspeaker, I almost vomited. Forcefully exhaling all my fear and panic, I tried to avoid making any sudden movement as I rose to my feet. The voice instructed me to enter the next room, where I would be thumbprinted. It sounded so matter-of-fact that my panic began to subside. In the next room, the air conditioner made me coo in relief and I went straight to the desk, where a lady sat with a machine designed to scan thumbprints. She was, disappointingly, a Pakistani, but she did have a vaguely American accent. She motioned for me to sit down and began typing on her keyboard.

The room was divided in half, with the all the visa applicants sitting on one side in plastic chairs that seemed specifically designed to damage the spine. On the other side of a glass partition were the Americans. I could see an American official (an actual honest-to-goodness American man) standing on his side of the glass, engaged in the world's most futile conversation – with an old Punjabi woman who couldn't speak a word of English but who had apparently claimed not to need a translator on the relevant part of her form. 'But why did you say you can speak English?' the American kept asking her with rapidly escalating frustration, to which the old woman would reply with increasing desperation that she couldn't speak English.

Their voices travelled through a metal sieve in the centre of the glass that separated them.

My nausea returned with a vengeance when I realised I was next in line to face this already-agitated embassy official who would probably have the deciding vote on my visa. I would never visit America and it would be this old woman's fault.

Why did she lie on her visa form? Why couldn't she learn English? Why did she want to go to America? I was focusing my hate like a laser on the old lady when the American dismissed her with a 'Thank you' that sounded not the least bit grateful. Then he called me up to the counter.

I bounced out of my seat with entirely too much manufactured enthusiasm and stood where instructed. An inch of bulletproof glass separated me from the first American I had ever met in person. A black man with perfect teeth and neatly trimmed short hair, he glanced at me once and then turned to a computer monitor.

'Name?' he said.

'Sami Shah.'

'Why are you going to America?'

'To study.'

'Where?'

'University of Virginia.'

'What?'

'Excuse me?'

'What will you study?'

'Computer science.'

'Hm.'

And that was it. That was all we ever said to each other. I wanted to say more, to tell him that I was fascinated by America and how I loved their Pamela Anderson, and that I understood how difficult it must have been for a black man to overcome a history of slavery and racism, and how I was against nuclear weapons. But none of that was necessary. He took my passport, stamped it and gave it back without ever looking up at me. And just like that, I was going to America.

16

The University of Virginia was established by Thomas Jefferson, one of America's Founding Fathers and its third president. As such, his shadow loomed large over the place, as though his DNA was mixed in with every building's concrete. Students referred to him as 'Mr Jefferson', a degree of familiarity afforded by paying the steep admission prices. The university wasn't a 'campus', it was 'The Grounds'; students weren't divided into freshmen, sophomores, juniors and seniors but 'first years, second years, third years and fourth years'. Apparently Mr Jefferson believed you could never be a 'senior' when it came to education.

Even the architectural style of the university buildings conformed to Mr Jefferson's personal fetish for Greek neoclassical structuralism. The heart of the campus – sorry, *The Grounds* – was the Rotunda, a replica of Mr Jefferson's own house, without the additional slave quarters in which he apparently had sex.

The campus was a sprawling expanse of low buildings spread out over the Virginia countryside, filling most of the town of Charlottesville. The buildings were almost all the same: red brick and, at their tallest, just three or four storeys high. Every building had a name chiselled over its entrance in very formal typography, commemorating wealthy alums who had donated money to build it or students who had gone on to achieve greatness (the most notorious being Cocke Hall and Balz House).

The American students we saw in movies never had such unique names, nor did they look as varied in appearance as those at UVa. The grounds thronged with students of all shapes and appearances. It was actually quite uncommon to see tall blondes with square jaws and steely eyes. Instead, I discovered, the average American would probably have dark hair and fair skin (tanned to a tomato red), be of average height and always have a stockier build than mine. The blond men stood out because they were rare. Blonde women were easier to find, as they tended to cluster together, roaming from building to building in breathtaking flocks.

The first time I truly understood what being in America meant, I had been at the university for two weeks. I was well settled into my dorm room, sharing it with Henry, an architecture major from Finland who taught me how to do shots, had much the same sense of humour as me and was always entirely too comfortable with nudity. I had grown so used to the university lifestyle – of classes, classes and more classes – that in just two weeks I felt as though I had been in America a very long time. The homesickness I had dreaded before arrival had surfaced only on my first night there, causing me to lie in bed staring at pictures of my parents until the sun came up. After that, I was just another busy first-year student.

On the day in question, though, I was reminded that America was quite different from home in very fundamental ways. September had just begun and the Virginia sun was providing the same kind of blast-furnace heat that I had hoped to leave behind in Karachi. Levi's-blue skies stretched for parsecs in every direction and I was sweating tremendously as I trudged back to my dorm from a Chemistry for Engineers class. I was reading a comic book as I walked and so didn't look up until I was very near the dorm building. Had I not looked up, I probably would have stepped on at least one glistening slender thigh and possibly fallen onto at least two pairs of perfect breasts. Fortunately I did look past the comic page and gave an embarrassingly audible gasp.

On the lawn in front of my dorm were half a dozen girls from the floor above mine, all lying down and baking under the sun. Their bikinis were soaked through with sweat and, as far as the erection that reared upwards in my pants was concerned, might as well not even have been there. Their attempt at tanning was being appreciated by all the boys in my building, who stood on the balconies and hooted and whistled. The girls, for their part, seemed to be ignoring the attention with minimal effort. I, for my part, neither hooted nor whistled. Instead I made a concerted effort to walk past them without staring too obviously, focusing instead on carrying my book bag in a casual way that concealed what must have been a monumental bulge.

It was only after I'd indulged all the fantasies my mind could furiously concoct – in which one or all of those girls decided they needed my help rubbing lotion on their breasts, after which there was some inevitable and joyous coupling – that I had time to meditate on the fact that I was indeed not in Karachi anymore. I had never seen that much female flesh revealed before, not in real life.

I could not have been happier.

Unfortunately, that happiness did not extend to my studies. Computer science majors had to spend their first semester studying the basics of science before being allowed to focus on the computer part. I hadn't studied science since ninth grade; after that the Cambridge system of education which my Karachi school subscribed to had forced me to choose between all-science and all-business subjects. I had chosen economics, commerce and accounting over physics, chemistry and biology. Now, five years later, I was completely lost in Chemistry for Engineers, Engineering Mathematics, Engineering Physics and Engineering Concepts. The only class I was doing reasonably well in was English for Engineers (which somehow was different from English for the Rest of the World). Everything else, I was failing spectacularly.

In the first laboratory assignment in Chemistry for Engineers, I managed to set my sleeve on fire and drop a tumbler full of acid on the ground. The maths class might as well have been taught in an entirely alien language and I gave up attending the Engineering Physics and Engineering Concepts classes altogether. It wasn't that I was frightened by the amount of work required; my brain just couldn't grasp the subject matter. While other students manipulated models of atomic structures and experimented with chemical bonding, I could barely get past basics like salt is salty. I had gained admission into the university of my choice, but I just didn't want to study what I had come there to study.

What I wanted to study, I realised, was how to become a writer. The university's English department was one of the best in America and within it, I decided, were the tools I needed to become an author. However, to transfer from computer science to English meant convincing my parents that I wasn't squandering the money they had spent sending me to university. It's much the same fight all English majors must have with their parents' expectations, except mine was made tenfold worse by being Pakistani.

All the other Pakistani students at the university were studying computer science or business. Those were subjects that guaranteed you a future of financial stability. You got a good degree, got a job and then got married. If you got a degree in something useless – like English, for example – you wouldn't get a job and then no one would marry you. I appreciated that my parents' conservative view of my future came from a place of genuine concern, but that didn't make my disagreement with them any less vehement. With every passing day, as my grades tumbled lower and lower, my conviction that I could one day be a great writer became more steadfast.

'We didn't send you there to study English,' my mother reasoned. 'If you have to waste your life, you can do that back here just as easily.'

'If I can't study English, then I might as well come back to Karachi anyway, because there isn't anything else I want to do,' I'd reply.

For most nights of that first semester, while everyone else went out and partied until they vomited or orgasmed, I paced The Grounds smoking cigarettes and furiously arguing with my parents in my head. The other Pakistanis I met at the university found my problem ridiculous; they agreed with my parents that taking an English degree was inherently irresponsible.

Eventually, when my first semester GPA (grade point average) dropped so low that the university put me on probation, my parents agreed to let me transfer to English. Over the next four years, I learned how to write short stories and develop a novel; I took courses on Shakespeare, Dostoevsky and Milton. I even wrote a terrible novel as my final-year thesis.

Although I didn't graduate with a publishing deal and a future as Pakistan's answer to Stephen King (my personal aspiration), I still don't regret my decision to change courses. Studying English meant I enjoyed studying for the first time in my life. Having transferred to the arts and sciences department in the university ('sciences' denoting 'social sciences', not hard science), I was able to take classes in other subjects as well. I studied the history of jazz, comparative religion, fine art and American politics. In summer I stayed on campus to take extra classes in subjects I wasn't able to get to during the regular terms, discovering sociology, art history, film theory and Islamic history. None of those courses helped me to get a job later in life, but all of them filled my head with new ideas and hitherto-unknown concepts, which made me better equipped to understand the world. It's a small consolation to my parents, who probably still wish I was a business analyst or computer programmer. But these days you're just as likely to find those two professions standing in the unemployment line as English majors.

17

America didn't disappoint. In every way, it lived up to its myths. Not just the promise of being whoever you wanted to be, which I was achieving by studying to be a writer, but also in the spectacle it promised. American movies showed a land glutted with sex and violence and both were on full display in my first year there.

During my semester as an engineering student – when I'd spend my free time marching all over the university, trailing a comet tail of cigarette smoke – Bill Clinton was facing impeachment for creatively using a cigar on an intern. Every day, the news would salaciously dissect exactly what President Clinton and the girl in the blue dress had done together and how it had affected his ability to perform as a president. For us Pakistanis it was hilarious. Our leaders committed brazen acts of corruption, shamelessly stealing from the nation and killing anyone who dared to criticise them, yet here American citizens were distraught over a sexual dalliance.

Then, a few months later, during my second semester at university, I returned from class one day to find every channel on TV hysterically reporting on the Columbine High shootings. Two teenage boys, armed with enough assault weapons to invade Afghanistan, had laid a path of blood and bullets through their high school.

In the ensuing weeks, Americans mourned the tragedy and hotly debated the causes. Video games were blamed, a Leonardo DiCaprio movie, music, even the corrupting influence of trench coats. Somehow, the fact that guns were easier to buy than basic medication never seemed to rate a mention. There have been many more shootings since then in America and the same debates play out each time. And every time, I remember watching the grainy helicopter footage of Columbine High and the pundits conducting acrobatic feats of logic to justify America's adoration of guns.

To me, at the time, all of this was fascinating. I watched American culture unfold around me, discovering it to be just as rich and complex as I had always imagined. I loved jazz, the blues, apple pie and gun nuts. For some reason, they resonated with me more deeply than my own culture of Islam, Bhangra music, masalas and more Islam.

Probably my happiest moments during that first year were when I'd walk to the local comic shop. In Karachi, my comic purchasing was limited to whatever random issues of random titles had been imported into the country that week. Bookstores would set aside for me a small pile of comics, which I bought weekly, and I had become adept at jumping into storylines midway and then imagining their conclusions after the subsequent titles in that particular series failed to arrive. But entire shops dedicated to comics and comic culture? That was the stuff of fantasies.

The nearest one to my dorm was five kilometres away, and every Wednesday I would walk to it after class. Its entrance was an unassuming door squeezed between a tattoo parlour and a Chinese restaurant; it opened onto a stairway leading downwards. The shop below was always dimly lit, and here a friendly man suffering from frightening obesity squatted behind the counter. He and I would spend an hour chatting about our favourite superheroes, then I'd leave with a stack of comics under my arm, reading them on the trek back. The fact that I remember those trips to the comic shop so vividly – in greater detail than the first time I drank alcohol or even lost my virginity – probably says a great deal more about me than I'd like.

At the start of my second year, a Pakistani friend asked me to tag along with him when he went for an interview. He was hoping to gain admission into a debating group. The Jefferson Literary and Debating Society was the most prestigious organisation at the university and he thought it would look great on his résumé. Admission was dependent on a rigorous interview, in which four members of the society assaulted you with questions on politics, history and American culture, and you were judged by the speed and eloquence of your response. I hadn't even heard of the society, but I went along to provide support and because I hadn't been fast enough to think of an excuse not to go.

The interview was inside Jefferson Hall, a Viking hall with dark wood panelling and tall windows. The walls were hung with paintings of famous past members, among them Woodrow Wilson and Edgar Allan Poe. At the far end of the room, too deep to be touched by sunlight, was an elevated stage. At its centre was an ornate leather chair and, on either side, desks. Facing the stage were fifty chairs, neatly arranged with an aisle down the centre.

I spent every Friday in that hall for the next three years and I still miss it more than anything else at the university. I was interviewed for the Jeff Society (as members referred to it) only because I was waiting for my friend to do his interview. He never got in, but I did. For the next semester, I attended the weekly meetings as a probationary, which meant I either had to successfully present a speech, read a short story or take part in a debate. At the end of the semester, my oratory and literary skills were evaluated by the regular members and I was then promoted to join their ranks.

In retrospect, I realise how silly it all must have looked. Instead of going to fraternity parties and getting drunk, every Friday at 7 pm the other Jeff Society members and I would dress formally, listen to a visiting lecturer and then engage in debates. This would go on till late into the night, with everyone referring to each other in the most formal terms possible. We were playacting at being adults and were probably all insufferably pretentious. But man, did I love it.

After a year in America, I had finally found my crowd. They valued writing and the eloquence of oratory as much as I did, and none of them was a business or computer science major. At worst we had a bunch of Law Schoolers in our ranks. The friends I made in Jeff Society are still the only friends from college I keep in touch with, and even though my wife cringes at my descriptions of those society evenings, I can think of no better way to spend a Friday night. It was at those weekly debates and oratory challenges that I learned how to talk on stage; this is what gave me any confidence I have as a stand-up comedian.

In my final semester, I won the most prestigious oratory award given by the society and my name was inscribed on a plaque still there inside Jeff Hall. I hope I can show that to Anya one day, even though she will probably roll her eyes at it. The Jeff Society motto, taken from Virgil's *Aeneid*, is *Haec olim meminisse iuvabit* – Latin for: 'In the future it will be pleasing to remember these things.' It is.

18

In my fourth year at UVa, I was living in an apartment off campus with two Pakistani friends, Omer and Irfan. I had settled so completely into life as an American college student that Pakistan itself seemed distant and vaguely alien. My mother would send me magazines in the mail every few months and we would pore over them as if they were artefacts, shaking our heads at how strange it must be to live back there. With graduation less than a year away, I was comfortably ensconced in a potential future in America. I had no idea what I'd do once the university spat me out, but I assumed I'd get a job writing for a magazine or website, be sponsored for a work visa and eventually apply for citizenship. It's certainly what my parents were hoping for and I was quite keen on that path myself.

I have always been nocturnal, never able to sleep until well into the night. Once everyone around me is asleep and the world quietens down, I revel in the silence – browsing the internet, reading comics and books, and generally filling my brain. As a result, I tried to avoid early-morning classes. The one time I had been unable to do so – having enrolled in a History of Islam class that began at 9 am – I fell asleep in the front row and was publicly berated by the professor.

So when Omer woke me early one morning to tell me a plane had crashed into a building in New York, I was too disoriented to grasp his meaning.

'Dude, check it out,' he said, 'it's all over the news. Some guy flew a plane into a building.'

Pulling on my glasses, I shuffled into the living room, where our other flatmate was standing with the television on. On the screen, CNN was showing footage of an ash-grey tower with black fingers of smoke pushing through it.

It took me several seconds to understand what was being shown. I had visited my uncle in New York a few months earlier and walked around Manhattan every day, so my memories of the World Trade Center were all from street level, looking up at those immense towers. CNN's view was almost level with the top of the buildings, with the focus on just one and the other entirely blocked from view by smoke.

'Is that the World Trade Center?' I asked.

'Yeah,' said Omer.

'What happened?'

'Some jackass flew a plane into it, I think.'

Still groggy from sleep, I turned away from the TV to go to the bathroom and wash.

'It's probably some amateur pilot,' I remember saying. 'I read something like that happened with the Empire State Building, like decades ago. Some guy flew a plane right into it.'

That's when the second plane appeared on the screen, darting behind the blazing tower. For an instant it disappeared from view; then an orange and red fist punched outwards.

'Holy shit, that's a second plane,' Omer said. 'A second plane just hit the towers.'

'That can't be an accident,' said Irfan, also watching.

On TV the anchors were still trying to understand what they were seeing. One argued that a plane had flown into the second tower as well, while the other insisted that it was just the fuselage from the original plane exploding. But we had seen it, had seen the plane enter the screen and the ensuing explosion.

We looked at each other and I said what we were all thinking: 'Please don't let it be Muslims.'

The idea of Muslims as perpetrators of terrorism predates 9/11, something that tends to be forgotten these days. The problem that now arose for the global Muslim community was that all the stereotypes they had been fighting against for decades were confirmed on that September morning in the eyes of the rest of the world. All the platitudes – that Islam is a religion of peace and Muslims aren't terrorists – crumbled along with the two towers.

As the towers burned, I threw on a jacket and ran across to where I knew my Jeff Society friends would be. On most days we all gathered in one of the connecting dorms that were occupied by the various society members. By the time I reached the dorm, a dozen of the regulars were already there, crowded around a small television set. When I walked in, they were taking it in turns to call friends and family in New York from the dorm phone.

I remember that, even though we were staring at the footage in horror, we made jokes. In retrospect, that seems like a horrific thing to have done, but at the time we just couldn't comprehend what we were seeing. The scale of the tragedy wasn't yet clear.

Even when one tower collapsed, it didn't seem real to us. I remember one friend from New York, watching the footage of the entire tower dropping down like an antenna being retracted, saying, 'It's like a special effect, right? It looks like a movie special effect. But not a good one. It looks fake. Doesn't it look fake?'

A few minutes later a girl in the group answered a phone call, and then turned to tell us that her father, who worked at the Pentagon, had just told her there had been an explosion there, but she shouldn't worry, because he was safe. Then the news began reporting that another plane had been hijacked. There were even reports of a car exploding outside the State Department, which later turned out to be false.

By late afternoon, it was over. The towers in New York had fallen; a plane had ploughed into the Pentagon; one more had smashed into a field in Pennsylvania. The US government grounded all flights across the country; news channels speculated as to the motivations behind the attacks, being careful to avoid guessing the identities of the attackers.

'People called from the planes, right?' a Jeff Society friend said. 'They made phone calls before the planes crashed. Well, I don't mean to sound insensitive, but Americans can be racist. If the hijackers were, y'know, brown, they'd mention it, right? Even if they were white, they'd say it.'

How I hoped the hijackers were white. At that point, every Muslim and every Middle Eastern and South Asian in the world was united in the same prayer: 'Please don't let them be brown. Please don't let them be Muslim.' If the hijackers turned out to be Timothy McVeigh-types, they would be individualised as insane. Muslims and brown people received no such consideration; if some hijackers shared our race or religious beliefs, then we were all hijackers. We were all terrorists.

I attended one class on 11 September, a creative-writing course. A dozen students sat at desks, unable to talk of anything but the attacks, until the professor walked in and told us there would be no classes that day. In the evening, a candlelight vigil was held on the footsteps of the Rotunda. Against a backdrop of Jeffersonian architecture, hundreds of students cupped their hands around softly dancing flames as the sun set. At night we began hearing the first stories of retaliatory attacks on Muslims across the country. My friends insisted on walking me home for the next few days and my mother called to check that I had shaved off the beard I had recently grown for purely aesthetic reasons.

The jingoism and patriotism that manifested after 9/11 was markedly aggressive in tone. In the early days after the attacks, President Bush actually stated that America would not invade Afghanistan, but someone had to pay: Americans demanded blood for their blood. Even cynical members of the intellectual fraternity I was proud to be a member of began saying things like, 'If saving one American means killing a thousand Afghanis, then that's what needs to be done.'

For the first few weeks after the attack, Pakistanis worried that the retaliation would be aimed at their homeland. I remember trying to convince my parents to grab my brother and sister and get on a flight to America. They had tourist visas already and they would be safer here than there. They refused, calling my concerns paranoid and overly dramatic, although I later learned that it was a genuine fear in Pakistan at the time.

American anger was further stoked when the news channels showed footage of Palestinians cheering the attack. Analysts bayed on television, demanding an explanation for the morbid celebrations. It was the first time America was confronted with the reality of how it was perceived beyond its borders, and anything less than complete sympathy was seen as unforgivable.

As the invasion of Afghanistan became inevitable, a counter-argument circulated, although it was never given mainstream coverage. Protestors marched in Washington DC, trying to reason for a measured response that wouldn't result in more civilians dying, even if those civilians lived in another country far away. I attended some of those rallies, and was even invited to speak on stage in front of the White House to several hundred protestors who pleaded for peace. It was the first time in my life that I began to feel the importance of political activism. Unfortunately, this awakening was countered by the uselessness of that activism. Despite President Bush's earlier assurances, America went to war with Afghanistan after all.

My reaction to the hysteria manifested in another, more peculiar way. I had never been very religious. I had taken courses on Islam in college in an effort to understand the attraction of the belief system my parents and everyone else back home subscribed to, but I didn't find its arguments convincing enough to fully embrace it myself. But after 9/11, it became clear that my personal beliefs didn't matter; I was going to be defined as a Muslim, based purely on my race and background, and I would thus be regarded with suspicion and fear. I got into arguments repeatedly, in classrooms and with friends, trying to prove that Islam advocated war and violence no more or less than any other religion, and that Muslims were not a single-minded hegemony. I was being forced into the role of an advocate of Islam, as were other brown people across America.

So, in retaliation, I became a practising Muslim. I don't know how much of this was an act of rebellion – fighting against cultural expectations by embracing the Other – and how much it was just me deciding to prove that all Muslims weren't terrorists by being a Muslim who wasn't a terrorist. I gave up drinking alcohol, a taste I had only acquired during my time in America, and began praying five times a day. I grew my beard back, and even visited the local mosque regularly. It's the only time in my life that I actually became actively religious and I couldn't have chosen a stranger time to do so.

This religious awakening, interestingly, lasted only as long as my time in America. Returning to Pakistan a year later, I was faced with the exact opposite attitudes. Not being a Muslim was considered an act of rebellion, and non-Muslims were persecuted. Confronted by the very problems with Islam that I had been trying to argue did not exist, and watching them dominate the national narrative of Pakistan, I reacted by turning atheist. As personal acts of rebellion go, I couldn't have chosen a more complicated way of exhibiting my individuality. I suspect my life would have been a lot easier if I'd just got an earring and done some drugs.

19

I graduated in the summer of 2002. In my four years in America, apart from seeing President Clinton get pilloried for a blowjob and teenagers walking through a high school with assault weapons and black trench coats, I had witnessed the pomp and pageantry of the 2000 US election, the early hilarity of the Bush years, followed by the traumatic events of 9/11 and the Afghan war that followed. In between, I'd had two disappointing relationships, ending in heartbreak (more for me than for the girls involved) and served as secretary of the Jefferson Literary and Debating Society (the same post Edgar Allen Poe had once held); I'd discovered how much fun getting drunk could be, and then renounced it when I had my religious awakening.

To finish my English degree, I'd been required to write a novel as my thesis project. By then I had written and published several short stories, but never attempted anything of that length. So, over two weeks, I smoked too many cigarettes, drank too many Red Bulls and typed until my hands cramped. The resulting book wasn't the homage to genre that I had always thought I'd write, but the semi-autobiographical story of a boy named Sameer Syed who visits Karachi during his summer vacations away from college in America. The entire thing was a testament to my growing uncertainty about whether to stay in the US, with deeply homesick descriptions of the city I hadn't visited in two years. It was also quite terrible.

With a bachelor's degree in my back pocket, I relocated to a suburb just outside Washington DC where a cousin lived; he let me stay with him until I found a job. I slept on his sofa for six months, finding neither an employer that would sponsor my visa, nor a publisher who could be persuaded to accept my novel. To be truly honest, I wasn't looking very hard for either.

While I decided what to do, I worked as a cashier at a bookshop close to my cousin's apartment. It was a small independent bookshop, the kind that doesn't exist in America anymore. I worked the evening shift, stacking books and organising shelves when not standing behind the cash register. It paid just enough money to keep me in movie tickets, cheap food and clothes. As well, the store manager let me borrow books, as long as I returned them within forty-eight hours. For the entire six months I held that job, I took two books every second day, read them in my free time and then exchanged them for two more.

It was a fairly blissful, if unsustainable, existence. However the area around my cousin's apartment was populated by young people with high-paying jobs, and I grew tired of seeing everyone else wearing nicer clothes and sporting newer and shinier accessories.

The short walk to the store and back was briefly rendered stressful when reports began appearing of a serial-killing sniper active in the area. Over three weeks in October, ten people were killed and three injured. At first it was believed this was a Muslim terrorist; then a white man with military experience in a white truck; but finally it turned out to be a black man with his teenage son in a blue Chevy. More even than 9/11, those attacks added menace to my daily life. One man was killed along the same route I took home, an hour after

I had passed by. I remember pushing my meagre stamina to its limits as I took to jogging home after my shift ended at 10 pm.

A few weeks before I quit my job and flew to Karachi, I was working the cash register at the shop when a man approached the counter with a stack of books. As I began to scan them, I noticed they were all related to Islam, terrorism and Osama bin Laden. Since 9/11, anything with even a whiff of those three subjects in the title was selling well enough to make a lot of heretofore forgotten academics extremely rich. As I ran the scanner over each book's barcode, the man, a blond-haired, blue-eyed type dressed in a suit, tried to engage me in conversation.

'Yeah, I've been reading a lot about bin Laden and Al-Qaeda recently.'

I just smiled and continued to scan.

Undeterred by my silence, he went on: 'I gotta say, I do agree with some of the things he says. Bin Laden, y'know. He makes some good points. What do you think?'

Ignoring the bait, I bagged his books, returned his change and thanked him for his patronage of the store. He gave up the curious line of questioning and left.

Many of my friends from university ended up working for the Pentagon and the State Department, UVa being close enough to Washington DC and the CIA headquarters in Langley to be a valuable recruitment centre. I called up a friend who had started working at the Pentagon and described the curious incident to her. She confirmed my suspicions.

'He was FBI,' she said. 'They've been casually investigating people that way for a while now.'

'That's the dumbest thing I've ever heard,' I said. 'What did he think? That I'd high-five him and invite him to join my personal Jihad against imperial forces right there in the bookshop?'

'Yeah,' she said. 'They aren't very bright.'

While the FBI agent's attempt at undercover questioning had been embarrassingly inept, it helped confirm my decision to return to Karachi. Even though my visa would last another year and so I had the option of returning, when I flew back in December 2002 I knew deep down that it was going to be for good.

America was feeling less like a place I could call home with every passing day. Karachi, I thought, would never stop being that. It would always be home.

I, KARACHI

20

As the plane descends, Karachi resolves like a polaroid developing. From above, the atomic substance of the city is brown: flat brown roofs, brown roads slicing across brown urban sprawl, with brown cars streaking across them. Even the sunlight looks like dust congealing. Heat bakes off the ground even before the plane lands, tyres squealing as they touch down on the sweaty tarmac. Exit the plane into Jinnah International Airport, walking past departure terminals caged in glass. The customs area is crowded already, multiple queues somehow all piled on top of each other. Arguments break out even before the first passport is processed – someone tries cutting in front, an old woman berates two young men, a young girl lectures an older man on his obvious lechery. A cat stalks the periphery, confidently herding arrivals with strangely human yowls. No one finds this odd. After half an hour of zombie-shuffling to the counter, a bearded man with a prayer mark on his forehead scans the passport, aims the eye of a webcam and then gives an approving nod. Porters sell their services around the trolleys like aggressive prostitutes, undercutting one another while trying to sneak a peek at luggage tags. The porters can be useful, however, for negotiating the phalanx of security personnel searching luggage for alcohol to be confiscated and resold. Step out into the car park; every pore instantly dilates in the humidity, the air suffused with sweat and exhaust. It used to be the airport was on the outskirt of the city, the road leading to it cutting across empty land, but Karachi is expanding so rapidly now you can hear it grow – a cacophony of musical bus horns, car bleats and rickshaw roars. The tidal pull of traffic swallows everything, dragging arrivals along in its swift undertow. There's no time to get overwhelmed; pausing to catch a breath would mean giving up a hard-earned place in the endless queue of vehicles. A motorcycle blazes past, its handlebar high-fiving other side-view mirrors, the rider sandwiched between his two children, his wife riding side-saddle behind them. A bus negotiates for space with all the diplomacy of a US president in talks with an oil-rich Middle Eastern despot; its passengers hang from its frame and tilt it like an elephant staggering under the effects of a tranquilliser. A Mercedes swerves to avoid being speared by iron rods hanging off the back of a donkey cart, forcing a rickshaw to screech sideways, its tyres scraping against the fractured pavement. Stay on Shahrah-e-Faisal long enough and everyone gets rear-ended, smashed, robbed and leered at. On the right is the naval airbase that was attacked by terrorists in 2011, where parked planes were gutted by grenades. Even on that day, the columns of smoke and fire, plus the military reinforcements rushing to the siege, did not slow the parade of traffic. A little further ahead, past the wedding halls and petrol stations offering compressed natural gas, is where Benazir Bhutto's convoy was attacked; the only memorial afforded the dead is a political-party flag stuck into the median strip. Turn right, abandoning the main road, and slow to a crawl on Karsaz Road, with its suburban congestion on the left and military bases across from them. Squeezing into a side lane to gather some momentum, the car bounces across a road that is just a collection of potholes stitched together with bits of tar.

I, MIGRANT

Up ahead is Kundun Broast, where chicken is deep-fried and pressure-cooked and served on the footpath – the stuff of expat dreams. Just before turning into the housing development, taking care to avoid the places where the road has collapsed entirely into the drains below, head for the Mohammad Ali Society neighbourhood. Here shops fringe a too-large roundabout – the Pak Medico clinic, where magazines were stolen when young; the Jumbo store, where they know every customer by name; a row of poultry and vegetable stalls, their patrons undeterred by the stink of the sewage that gels across every surface as gutters burp out black water, as they have for years. The movie shop is still on the corner, transitioning from VHS to LCD to DVD over the years (pornos can be bought with a wink and a nudge). Kaybee's still sells swirly ice-cream cones in the same three flavours, even though the place is now two storeys high. Their mango smoothies are still squeezed out the front and have a dedicated following, despite the fog of flies around each glass. One lane behind here is Ponderosa, the South Indian restaurant whose customers long ago decided the food was so good they didn't care about the cat-sized rats perched on neighbouring tables. Besides, the rats probably have lung cancer from inhaling the apple-flavoured sheesha smoke that coils over the entire lane. Head out of Mohammad Ali Society, grabbing a samosa or three from the bakery and trying to eat them all while winding through the web of streets leading home. Even this far away, Shahrah-e-Faisal traffic creates a din that hangs over everything, punctuated by the wail of ambulance sirens. Five times a day, multiple mosques – all within walking distance of each other – add to the orchestral mess with the call to prayer blaring over megaphones. Staying on Shahrah-e-Faisal for a little while longer, on the right is the swish neighbourhood of PECHS (Pakistan Employees Cooperative Housing Society). More suburban glut, with schools interspersed among the houses. An entire childhood can be spent ricocheting between those schools – one to start at, one to get expelled from and one to finish in. Back on the main road, the sludge of traffic moves on, past office buildings and windowless apartments, all painted the same exhaust-grey. The only splash of colour comes from advertising billboards, screaming messages of commerce every few feet. GOOD MORNING LIFE WITH OLPER'S MILK! . . . I WEAR ASIM JOFA! . . . FREE MUGS WITH LIPTON! . . . SILKY SOFT SKIN BY LUX! . . . STUDY IN UK! . . . APPLY NOW! . . . FREE! . . . SALE! . . . DISCOUNT! . . . NOW! Overpasses cast wedges of blue shadow, leading off into other parts of the city. That way is Goli Mar, where the O-level exams were conducted in the 1990s while gang wars blazed right outside the walls. Go in the other direction, past the graveyard where the British Raj buried their dead – their interred bones the last physical remnants of colonial history – and come to the Kala Pul bridge that for so long was the dividing line between Karachi's rich and poor. In the end Karachi's rich retreated and now even this bridge finds itself marooned among the impoverished masses, its footpaths providing lodgings for junkies, who shoot their veins full of heroin under the apathetic glare of the day. Shahrah-e-Faisal curves ahead in the distance, one last time before it ends, smacking into the hollowed skull of the old Hotel Metropole. In the sixties there were nightclubs here; jazz bands performed for women in minis and waiters served wine and champagne. All that remains now is a cracked facade around a car park. Sitting in front is the same old man who has been sitting here for decades, selling polished brass antiques salvaged from a graveyard of ships. On the other side is the entrance to a restaurant that was once famous for its chicken tikka and is now only remembered as the last place Daniel Pearl was seen alive. The road splits around the old Metropole. Turn this way and you end up in Saddar, where

Victorian-era buildings, blackened with age and neglect, have been repurposed into shops that sell everything you'll ever need, as long as you can find parking. Go straight on and drive past the entrance to the Sind Club, where the too-rich gather to celebrate their wealth under mahogany fittings and oil paintings. Across the road is the Karachi Gymkhana, another private club that is no longer considered prestigious. Up until the 1940s, a sign outside read: DOGS AND MUSLIMS NOT ALLOWED. These days even the dogs can get in without a membership card. Further on are two five-star hotels, their entrances fortified with concrete blocks and metal containers – every car is strip-searched before entry. Go the other way, however, and a narrow road takes you past the hulking remains of what was once the US consulate; beyond that is a dusty cathedral surrounded by neatly manicured lawns, which no one is allowed to walk on, and one more heavily guarded five-star hotel. Then on to Clifton. Over a bridge, under another bridge, past the statue of three marble swords – with the words UNITY, FAITH and DISCIPLINE carved into them without any discernible sarcasm intended – and from there on it's nothing but towering shopping malls and roadside food stalls. Buy a Burberry handbag and eat a greasy bun kebab. Get an iPhone, and then have it stolen while enjoying a plate of butter chicken. There are still some old houses left here; the inches of dirt settled on them can be carbon-dated to the early years of the last century. One of those houses, hidden behind pistachio walls higher than the building itself, is where Benazir Bhutto's brother lived; a portrait of him still adorns the wall facing the road. His painted eyes look out towards the place where he was shot to death one night – rumour has it by his sister's husband. But no one slows down long enough to consider this morbid nugget of information as they speed past the barbed-wire gates of the British Council compound, ignoring the suspended pirate ship swinging in a pendulum arc in Fun Land and, beyond it, the mall shaped like a concrete sail. Until they run right into the Indian Ocean. Because that's where Karachi ends, for now. Grey water barricades the city, at least until more land is dredged up and Karachi expands even further out, trying to find more room for its millions. Yet even this drive, close to two hours from airport to seafront, barely hints at the size of the city. Shahrah-e-Faisal and the localities that fringe it are just the thin spine that runs through Karachi. Spreading out around it are wings of concrete and mud, miles upon miles of thatched slums and urban decay. It isn't called a city anymore; it's too large to be properly defined by the same word that is used to describe places so small by comparison. Now it is a mega-city. It would be more appropriate to call it the 'Infinity City', or even 'Ur City'. Whatever you call it, Karachi grows and spreads – a megalopolis that holds on to everything. No matter how far away you go to escape it.

21

I'm a Karachiite first, then a Pakistani. If it seems strange that I identify myself with a city more than the country within which that city is situated, then you haven't met many people from Karachi. The city is so large, its personality so overwhelming and its persecution complex so deeply embedded that almost everyone who lives there distrusts anyone who doesn't. There is a unique pride associated with coming from Karachi; its denizens walk around with an attitude that says, 'I'm from Karachi and I'm not dead yet.' Then they get robbed at gunpoint.

Like most Karachiites, my family originated somewhere else. My mother's side of the family started in Iran, then moved to India. In 1947, shortly after Pakistan sprang from India's ribs, my maternal grandfather visited some friends in Karachi for a New Year's Eve party. They convinced him to skip his return flight to Bangalore and stay an extra day. It was fortunate that he did, because the plane he was scheduled to take crashed. Taking this as a divine message, he settled in Karachi.

I don't remember him; he died when I was a little over two years old. My mother tells me I used to walk with him in the garden every day; everyone who knew him and has met me says I have his sense of humour. He must have wielded it with more charm and charisma though, since everyone who knew him loved him a great deal. A portrait of him still hangs in the drawing room of our family home – a dark man with a hairline that had all but surrendered hope of existence and thick spectacles perched on a nose prominent enough to require its own separate portrait. That nose is the other thing he apparently handed down to me, although I am less grateful for it, despite my mother's assurances that it is a sign of greatness.

He had many children, because back then if you were a virile male you didn't just stop at five. My mother was the youngest of the brood and so she learned to fight for her place from almost the moment she was born. She describes the Karachi of her childhood as entirely different from the one I grew up in, with weekly horseraces, courtly galas and an environment of casual safety that would seem alien to any modern Karachiite.

Other than being a wit and the owner of a prodigious nose, my grandfather was also a hugely successful businessman who owned printing presses, real estate and two hotels. Of course, as luck would have it, all that was gone by the time I was born, sold off so my grandfather could leave each of his children an equal share of his fortune, thus preventing them from squabbling over their inheritance. But during my mother's childhood, the wealth that came with those business successes was taken for granted. She and her siblings still tell stories of running amok in their father's hotel and attending races dressed in their finest clothes.

Shortly before my mother was born, my grandfather built the house in which I also would grow up and in which Anya, my daughter, was born. A three-storey building, it is shaped like a curved rectangle and has almost a dozen rooms, each separated by a foot of concrete so impenetrable that it is still the bane of every plumber and electrician called to work on it. The house offered two separate gardens and a snaking driveway. Over the years, as siblings moved away and inflation moved up, my parents struggled to maintain the place, eventually offering half of it out for rent.

It was in that house that my parents met for the first time. My father's family was also transplanted from India, but chose to base themselves in Lahore. My paternal grandfather worked as a civil servant in Punjab, his job requiring him to constantly move from posting to posting. As a result, my father, along with his four younger siblings, grew up in boarding schools, spending most of his childhood in Abbottabad, where decades later Osama bin Laden would settle down with three wives and a treasure trove of porn.

When my father turned eighteen, his father sent him to join the merchant navy, because back then you didn't ask your children what they wanted to do, you told them what they were going to do. From his days as a cadet to when he eventually retired as a captain more than forty years later, my father spent almost every day of his adult life at sea, something no one had ever asked him if he was particularly interested in doing.

After my parents were joined in an arranged marriage, my mother stayed home in Karachi while my father sailed, often absent for several months at a time. Fortunately, he was on shore leave when I was born a year later. My mother went into labour at night and was rushed to the nearest hospital, which happened to be closed. Because the second-nearest hospital was across the city in those days, my father scaled a drainpipe at the closed hospital, shimmied across several thin ledges and frightened a gaggle of off-duty nurses by thumping on the window of their office, three storeys above the ground. I was born the next afternoon and still wonder if I was worth all the trouble.

Every male on my father's side of the family is broad-shouldered, tall and strikingly handsome, with chiselled jawlines and arms thick with muscle. Every male on my mother's side is also tall, but mostly skinny with immense noses and failing eyesight. I, of course, got most of the maternal genetic detritus. During my childhood, aunties and uncles teased that I should carry stones in my pocket, in case I was blown away, and that my nose was large so as to balance the weight of my spectacles, just as a brontosaurus's tail keeps it from tipping over. Pakistani aunties and uncles can be arseholes.

My paternal grandmother was thrilled with me, though, since I was the fairest child ever born into her family. For the first year of my life, I had skin so pale that I was mostly an X-ray and I also had unnaturally blond hair. In South Asia, which never recovered from the Western aesthetics imposed on it by centuries of British rule, having fair skin and light hair were like being born holding a winning lottery ticket. I have yet to deflate from the adoration I received in those first years of my life.

However, because the world is cruel and the sun shines down on all of us, my skin and hair eventually darkened. The resultant disappointment – coupled with the fact that I was growing up so skinny catwalk models would envy me and I couldn't see past the first few inches of my nose without spectacles – has left me with a perpetual complex about my physical appearance. It was only recently pointed out to me that anger and revulsion aren't natural responses to looking in the mirror. Worried by the constant gibes of 'He's so skinny' and 'Don't you feed him anything?', my mother would take me to the doctor regularly. My paediatrician was a kindly old Zoroastrian lady named Dr Mama; she would listen to my mother's anxieties, then cluck disapprovingly and say, 'When they say he's skinny, na, you should say, "Yes, but he is healthy," na.'

I marvel at people who have vivid memories of their early child-hood. I've read autobiographies by writers who describe their first cogent thoughts, their first conversations and the first time they fell over. I only have fleeting glimpses at best; any memories I have of my childhood are falsely constructed out of second-hand anecdotes.

Apparently one of my first words was a curse word. That my father and his friends swore like sailors can be forgiven, since they were all actual sailors. One day, while sitting on his lap and listening to his friends talking, I finally decided to contribute by parroting the only word that had been repeated continually in the conversation. Slapping my thigh, I laughed and said, 'Sister Fucker!'

My mother is still not amused by this story. Nor does she have particularly fond memories of when, at the age of three, I was taken to the doctor for a routine check-up and the clinic confused my medical report with that of a much older patient with the same name. That man was given a report saying he had a mild flu and should drink lots of water, while I was described as being in the advanced stages of lung cancer with just a few weeks left to live. Relatives abroad were called and the report read out to specialists in America and London, who all concurred that my demise was unavoidable and deeply tragic for one so young. Never one to pass up the chance to add unnecessary drama to an already dramatic situation, a few days into the panic I looked up at the sky and said to my mother, 'What a beautiful sky, Mummy! Will I ever see a sky that beautiful again?' My parents wept.

A week later, when we returned to the hospital for another check-up, the doctor confessed to the mix-up and apologised for any trauma it might have caused us. I feel bad for the man who got my report by mistake. I hope he spent his last few days in blissful ignorance.

Other than those two stories, the only other memories I have are fragmented, like the shards of a broken mirror reflecting disconnected images: standing on the bridge of my father's ship when he took us with him once, and watching the ocean churn around us; crying because my parents wouldn't buy me an E.T. doll whose finger lit up, which I saw in a shop in Antwerp when the ship docked there for a day; being pinched mercilessly by my cousin Sara, who was two months younger than me and always brutally dominating; sitting in the back seat of our Volkswagen Beetle as we ate peach melbas across from the Hotel Metropole; and reading. More than anything else, I remember reading. My mother taught me to love books early on. By the time I was four, she had taught me to read in English and I had worked my way through the adventures of Peter and Jane, who spent a lot of time looking and seeing.

'Look, Peter, look. Look at the dog.'

'See, Jane, see. See Peter looking at the dog.'

Riveting stuff.

By the time I was five and my sister was born, I had a meticulously maintained collection of early readers – books about enormous turnips, lions and mice, and the tragic downfall of Jack and Jill – and was graduating to Enid Blyton's stories.

By the time of Safieh's arrival, I had spent enough time as the centre of parental and grandparental adoration to be magnanimous in relinquishing it to her. That it was then taken from her four years later and focused on my younger brother, Azmat, isn't my fault. Nor did I begrudge the fact that, unlike me, they both got better servings of the genetic soup. When she was born, Safieh already weighed almost as much as I did as a five-year-old; she had thick curly hair and almost immediately started winning prizes for academic brilliance. Azmat has my father's chiselled jawline, an ability to make his hair do whatever he wants it to (mine has always remained defiantly independent of my wishes) and a deep, gravelly voice, in stark contrast to my testicle-vibrating pitch.

Wanting to become a writer is one of the few moments in my life I remember with clarity. I was ten years old and my mother had decided the bookshop near the house was too limited in its offerings to sustain my reading habit. By this point, she had surrendered to the fact that there was nothing else I liked doing other than reading. Family dinners, weddings and even my own birthday parties were all spent with me sitting in a corner, bony knees drawn up and giant spectacles trained on a book in my lap. I had already earned a reputation in the family for disappearing into the bathroom for an hour at a time, sitting naked on the toilet with a book until my legs went numb. (I recently tried a meditation exercise to help me with anxiety, which required me to visualise the one place in which I might find complete calm and serenity. Instantly, my mind formed an image of the bathroom I spent most of my childhood in, perched on the porcelain seat with a book in my lap. Elvis died on the toilet. If he was anything like me, it was a happy death.)

To encourage me to move beyond the Hardy Boys and *The Magic Faraway Tree* I was obviously outgrowing, my mother got us membership to the Karachi Gymkhana. An old private club that predated the existence of Pakistan, it had tennis courts, a cricket stadium and catered food. I only really cared about the library though. Rows and rows of books inside a huge room where everyone sat in reverential silence. I was limited to three books at a time, a frustration I overcame by persuading my mother to borrow books for me under her name.

I remember one of my cousins asking me once, 'Why do you read so much?' At the time, I couldn't articulate a proper answer, not being able to understand the question. I think I replied with something snippy like, 'Why don't you read as much?' Maybe I read because, what with the spectacles and the lack of muscle mass, I was terrible at sports. All my friends played cricket every day and the few times I joined in, I was grudgingly chosen last to join the team. Or maybe I read because there wasn't much else to do. TV offered very little back then, nor was there much else for young boys to do in Karachi other than riding a bicycle around town or playing video games, both of which I had tried and found boring.

But, in the end, I think my original answer is still the most appropriate. When I read, it's a wholly immersive experience. Dull reality dissolves the moment I open the cover of a book and, if the story being told is compelling enough, it dissolves all other problems. When you're riding alongside a dragon or fighting a horde of Orcs, you don't worry about missing your father or the report cards filled with red ink your teachers keep sending home or how everyone calls you skinny. Why would you not want to read all the time?

The first book I borrowed from the Karachi Gymkhana library was Ursula K. Le Guin's *A Wizard of Earthsea*. Until that book, magic and fantasy was just something that happened in books about magic and fantasy. Dragons existed; people waved their hands and made things appear or change; and it was all arbitrarily harmless and entertaining. In her Earthsea trilogy, though, Le Guin crafted rules for magic, dragons came with consequences and even names bore arcane weight. I read that first book over and over again in a single week, then decided I wanted to write one just like it. With a discipline that my teachers would have found impossible to believe, I penned an entire fantasy book over the next few days, writing in a school exercise book.

It was, of course, a completely terrible copy of *A Wizard of Earthsea*, involving an orphaned boy who discovers it is his destiny to become the greatest wizard of all time and rides around on his pet dragon chasing his enemies. All of that happened in the first chapter, I think.

I don't remember much else of that book, but I do remember relishing every word I wrote.

'Mummy,' I said, presenting it to her, 'I'm going to become a writer.'

I think she would have preferred it if I had said doctor or lawyer or banker. But, to her credit, she didn't dissuade me. Mostly because the week before I had said I wanted to be a musician, and the week before that a gynaecologist (I had meant to say archaeologist).

'That's nice,' she said. 'Now please finish your homework.'

22

Having a father who was only at home for two or three months a year was a strange thing to grow used to, especially for my siblings. Before Safieh was born, my mother and I had gone with him on the ship twice, sailing around the world for several months at a time. My memories of those trips are vague and consist almost entirely of vomiting.

Back then, he would be gone for a couple of months at a time, with the breaks in between just as long. His absences increased gradually for me, a month being added with every promotion. It became a routine part of my life – not having him there for extended periods of time, with the only contact being a long-distance phone call he managed whenever the ship docked long enough for him to get shore leave. Besides, he would return with gifts, unpacking suitcases to give me action figures and chocolates. As a child, I was shallow enough to have any yearning for him placated with the promise of eventual presents.

By Safieh, he was up to six months at a stretch, and by Azmat, he had been promoted to chief officer and he was now away for nine months with two months between voyages. Desperate to spend time at home with his family, he made several attempts to find a shore job; but, having been sailing since he was eighteen, he knew nothing else.

My mother, as a result, was cast in the role of single parent in charge of three children. Safieh and Azmat proved worry-free. Azmat was too young to do anything other than gurgle and fill his nappy. Safieh, on the other hand, was a model child, splitting her time between piano lessons and winning medals for being Student of the Year. I, however, decided that having the burden of being the man of the house placed on my narrow shoulders at such a young age meant I could start failing every subject at school.

A cycle developed which began with my teachers complaining to my mother that, though I was bright, I was refusing to apply myself in class. My mother would then confiscate my comics, hide all my action figures and complain to my father when he called. He would lecture me over the phone; I'd apologise and promise to try harder. And so I would, but only long enough to get my comics and action figures back; then it was time for the cycle to repeat itself.

It wasn't that I didn't understand what was being taught; I just couldn't bring myself to care. For me, time wasted studying could be better spent reading comics and fantasy novels and drawing superheroes. I'd already decided that, when I grew up, I was going to become a writer, so learning algebra or how much snow fell over the Karakoram Range wasn't really relevant to me.

I realise now that my mother was lax in her punishments. But she wasn't to blame; she was bringing up three children single-handedly in a giant house that required constant maintenance. That none of us is a drug-addled criminal with abandonment issues is a credit to her dedication and nurturing.

When I was ten years old, my father – for reasons he has yet to adequately explain – bought a rooster, some hens and a pair of geese. Every time he returned from a voyage, he would bring us presents from the far-off lands he had visited; maybe this one time he felt the chocolate boxes and action figures weren't enough, and so he supplemented them with some poultry. We came home from school one day to see him proudly standing over a small collection of beaks and feathers. My brother and sister were too young to care about the new additions to our household and, in my defence, I did try to like them. However, when approached, the geese showed themselves to be feral creatures capable of intimidating a pit bull. They would lower their necks, spread their wings and hiss like snakes as they charged across the garden towards me.

A couple of days later, they were discreetly driven to a pond across the city and left there. I was too young to read the newspaper back then, but I'm sure stories began appearing about innocent Karachiites assaulted by a pair of thuggish geese. They're probably holding high political office by now.

The chickens were harmless as chickens go, but the rooster became my enemy almost right away. Large by rooster standards and with a proud bearing, in front of everyone else in the family he would strut and crow entertainingly. But whenever he saw me alone, he would turn from pet rooster to clawed fury. Maybe he sensed my physical weakness or perhaps he just hated bookish geeks. Any chance he would get, the plumed bastard would charge at me and begin pecking at my wafer-thin shins. I began to avoid going into the garden, surrendering the outdoors to him.

Unfortunately, I let down my guard one day when my mother asked me to collect the mail from the letterbox by the gate. I was probably reading at the time – when I read I enter a fugue state in which I will carry out any orders given, so long as they don't require me to look up from the book – and so I walked outside, my field of vision blocked entirely by pages of text. So deep was my meditative condition that I didn't even register the first two pecks. When I finally looked down, the damned creature had stabbed my foot so many times with its arrowhead beak that the surface of my marble-white skin was stippled with blood.

I shrieked, swatted at the rooster with my book and then ran back to the house, the beast giving chase. The entrance to the kitchen could only be reached after climbing four large steps. I slipped on the second one, hitting the top one forehead first. The cook came outside just in time to see a dazed boy sitting on the ground with blood gushing from his forehead as a rooster pecked at his shoulder. Thinking quickly, the cook wrapped a towel around my head and called out to my mother, who paled by several shades and then screamed for my father.

As we drove to the hospital, my mother lectured my father on the poor judgment involved in bringing killer roosters into the same house as unsuspecting children. A doctor applied several stitches to the cut and recommended a few days of bed rest. After we returned home – my head heavily bandaged and my mother still delivering her full-throated lecture – my father had the rooster killed, plucked and served for dinner.

23

Though large, our house was never empty. While our family lived in one half, the other half was always occupied by others. For the first decade or so, it was another sailor like my father, together with his wife and three children. After they moved out, my father's younger brother and cousin moved in.

As a result, the house was always noisy, always full of visitors and still large enough for everyone to have their own room. At that age, I was grateful for the constant company and my mother was no doubt grateful for any help she got in taking care of the children. It was only after I hit puberty that I began to yearn for the privacy that was growing hard to find.

--------- • ---------

I've always had a strange relationship with porn. I talk about porn in my stand-up, but then you'd be hard-pressed to find a comedian who doesn't. When I first started writing jokes about porn and masturbation, I genuinely thought I was breaking new ground – a perverted Neil Armstrong sticking his penis into the moonscape of Pakistan's collective unconscious. It was only after moving to Australia and meeting other comedians in open-mics and comedy clubs that I realised how ubiquitous a topic porn is. Male comedians, at least, rarely consider their set complete without a healthy ten-minute chunk on masturbation. But, in my solitary experience as a stand-up comic in Pakistan, I was convinced that I was challenging the status quo in some way.

I received an email from an Australian once that showed me how strangely the rest of the world perceives Pakistani attitudes towards sex. This was around the time when I had been invited to attend the comedy festival on Sydney Harbour. Until the Australian embassy decided the national security of their nation could not be risked by allowing a skinny Pakistani comedian entry, a poster with my name and email address had been plastered all over the festival website. Most of the emails I received were fairly sweet and innocuous – genuinely surprised Australians writing to tell me they'd never known there was stand-up comedy in Pakistan, which was a reasonable reaction.

Then I got one from a woman who convinced me people outside Pakistan had no idea about the country. The writer had followed a link to a YouTube clip of me performing some of my searingly innovative porn-based comedy in a Lahore college auditorium. She wrote: 'I didn't realise Pakistanis had sex.'

First, let me dispel any confusion: Pakistanis do, indeed, have sex. We do not rely on some black market cloning technology for reproduction purposes, nor do we spawn from magical pools of amniotic goo, like the Orcs in *The Lord of the Rings*. Indeed, some Pakistanis have quite a bit of sex. Others have less than they would like. The men have sex with women; the women have sex with men (although I doubt their experience is anywhere near as satisfying). Sometimes the men even have sex with other men, although discussing or acknowledging that probability is actively discouraged. In rare cases (but not rare enough), they have happily stuck it in animals as well. Some years ago, the national newspapers reported on a man being discovered in the act of lovemaking with a donkey. Unfortunately, the donkey belonged to his neighbour. Because this took place in a village, a tribal council was quickly convened and both the man and the donkey were judged guilty of dishonouring themselves. The donkey, in keeping with rural customs, was killed; the man escaped, both village and his death. I wish I was making some of this up – I remember being quite depressed about the poor donkey's tragic death, although not as depressed as the man must have been.

Social and governmental prohibitions have tried desperately to limit and control all discussion of sex. Pakistan has an extremely Victorian sensibility when it comes to carnal acts: while we are aware that people regularly get naked and push their genitals against each other, we don't think it's something that we need to be reminded of. Much like nose-picking, sex should be done in private – preferably at home, with no one watching. And never in the car.

Attempts at censorship are generally a futile exercise, though. Lust, particularly male lust, runs to depths that can never be plumbed. Women may think they have an idea of how deep it goes, but they don't. Even we men don't. Our hunger for sex goes so deep, it frightens even us – beyond where the light can reach, below standard lechery and urges, below even fetishes and deviance, it is at such a depth that the pressures crush all comprehension and coherent thought. That is where monsters dwell. Horny creatures that can never be catalogued, nor understood. Frightful denizens of our lusty ocean floor. And so, even in the most constricting of societies, sex finds a way to flourish.

All the way up to the late 1980s, sex was cut out of every Hollywood movie before the Pakistani public were permitted to view it. Not even a kiss made it past the censors. The hero and heroine would lean towards each other, lips parting and eyes closing . . . Then suddenly they were enjoying a post-coital cigarette. What happened in between was a mystery. However, extreme violence was left uncensored. We were believed to be more capable of dealing with a still-pulsing heart being pulled out of a man's chest than lips brushing. That is why we Pakistanis are quick to commit violence and slow to love.

While I was growing up, there were only two TV channels. One was the state-run channel, PTV, which was fanatically regulated. During the dictatorship of Zia Ul Haq, a woman couldn't appear on screen without her head covered. Even in dramas featuring scenes of women waking in the morning, the characters rose from their beds with scarves already firmly fastened in place.

Then, during Benazir Bhutto's prime ministership, the shawls loosened; as they moved further back on the head, puffs of hair emerged from underneath. When the more conservative government of Nawaz Sharif followed shortly afterwards, the shawls crawled back up to their original positions. It got so that you could tell who was in power by the way the PTV female newscasters wore their hijabs.

The other channel at this time only broadcast in the evenings but, when it debuted in 1990, it was seen as a revolution in TV programming. The entertainment-deprived children of Pakistan got to watch a half-hour of cartoons, uninterrupted. Every day brought us the adventures of anthropomorphic warrior cats or space-faring cowboys, followed by ancient British comedies and topped off with an hour of the most notorious failures in US drama history.

But we were not ungrateful. To us, shows like *Manimal* (a man who fought crime by changing into either a panther or a falcon), *The Wizard* (a midget who built toys that always matched his adventurous needs perfectly) and *Street Hawk* (like *Airwolf*, except with a motorcycle) were the greatest things we had ever seen. We spent hours discussing the practical logistics of how *Manimal* could change into an elephant if need be; to this day if you see any motorcyclist going too fast in Pakistan, people refer to him as a 'Street Hawk'.

Years later, when the internet informed me that these shows were actually considered failures in America, I felt betrayed. While American children were watching better shows with better stories and better heroes, we had been donated the damaged and expired stuff. Much of the breakdown in Pakistan and American diplomacy can be traced to this unhealed wound in our collective psyche.

Then satellite dishes erupted into our sociocultural landscape. Within a few months, every household I knew had installed a large fibreglass bowl with an antenna sticking out the middle. All of a sudden television had become the centrepiece of a cultural revolution. CNN and BBC broadcast twenty-four-hour news that gave us the outside world's perspective on Pakistan; music channels taught us pop, rap, rock and R&B; and Indian channels showed us the enemy was just like us (in that they also watched terrible soap operas about the endless wars between mothers- and daughters-in-law).

And then there was *Baywatch*.

Given what I have just said about the depths of our collective sexual frustration, the effect of those swimsuit-clad buxom bomb-shells shouldn't come as a surprise. Overnight, Pamela Anderson and her cohorts jiggled and bounced their way into our lives. Parents suddenly had to guard children from the television, and children had to guard against their parents catching them watching said television. Moral authorities were up in arms and, if the shrill panic in every social moderator's voice was to be believed, we were on the brink of societal collapse, brought about by slow-motion jogging. The impact on us teenagers – struggling to stay focused on impending examinations – was catastrophic. We couldn't have been more distracted if we had been told to solve differential equations in a strip club. In unison, Pakistani boys tossed aside their textbooks and grabbed their penises.

For me, Pamela Anderson's arrival was almost perfectly timed to coincide with the discovery of masturbation. It was all my friends and I talked about – endless discussions, conducted in hushed tones during lunch breaks at school, as we reverentially shared fabricated wisdom with each other. We were in the throes of puberty and all around us girls were sprouting breasts.

Unfortunately for us boys, we countered those wondrous mutations with itchy underarms and painfully constant erections. For us it was torture; for the girls, as far as we could tell, it was highly amusing. And so every day, during lunch break, we would form a protective huddle and talk about the single greatest shared achievement in our lives.

'I read in my dad's medical books that every time you masturbate you lose a pint of blood,' expounded one boy. His father was a doctor, and so he was our resident authority on all medical matters. 'That means if you masturbate more than twice a day, you could die.'

'Fuck,' said another with a look of horror on his face, 'I masturbated four times last night.'

'You should have orange juice quickly,' offered the medical expert.

'You know, if you masturbate more than a hundred times in your life, you get AIDS,' announced another prodigy. This was followed by a long moment of silence as each boy did some panicked maths.

Finally, I worked up the nerve to ask, 'What's AIDS?'

'Oh, it's a disease that makes you gay. And everyone you touch becomes gay as well.'

'Shit,' said another. 'I think my cousin has AIDS then. He plays with dolls.'

'Don't touch him,' we advised.

And so on. Each day brought some new bit of information about how masturbation could kill you and each night we all worked hard at separating fact from myth. By the end of seventh grade, had the stories been true, my school would have been struck by an epidemic that attacked only boys, leaving them emaciated husks who played with dolls, had fur on their palms and penises that had been worn down to tiny withered nubs.

Back then we had no easy access to pornography. This was still a pre-internet world, in which porn was hard to acquire and hoarded jealously. For two years after I turned eleven, I owned one single porn film – a VHS I had received from a friend whose house was not porn-safe, due to a father who didn't respect the privacy of his pubescent son. I watched that tape over and over, night after night. By the time I was thirteen, I knew every grunt and squeal by heart.

When I found myself growing bored with the single VHS porno I possessed, I asked friends for more, but no one was ready to surrender theirs. So I drew some.

I've always enjoyed drawing. Having discovered comic books years before, I had filled many sketchbooks with detailed renderings of muscular heroes eye-blasting alien menaces while scantily clad women pranced around them. As I grew more and more desperate for something new to inspire my masturbation, I realised that the scantily clad women were a great deal more fun to draw than the muscular hero or his enemy. Except, that is, for when I drew the muscular hero and the scantily clad woman having sex.

I filled page after page with carnal battles. I would draw late into the night, studiously mastering the rules of anatomy and musculature for my own deviant purposes. Within a few weeks I had several hundred pages filled with graphite copulations – thick sketchbooks crammed inside my cupboard drawers under a camouflage of socks and underwear. And if I had left them there, everything would have been all right.

I'll admit to pride. There was definitely some of that involved in my decision to take those drawings to school and show them off to my friends. I thought they were really damned good works of art. The shading and tonal values in some of them were beyond anything I had done up to that point.

But there was also genuine altruism involved. I actually thought I had come up with a solution to our porn deficit. If someone comes up with a viable alternative to fossil fuel, would that person not want to share their discovery with the world? I simply wanted to provide much-needed relief to the pornographic famine we were suffering. So I stuffed the drawings into my bag and took them to the school with me . . . on the very day that the teachers announced a random bag check.

They hadn't been tipped off. It's not like someone had warned them about a teenage boy smuggling contraband smut into the classroom. No, it was just bad luck on my part. Terrible luck, really. Someone had stolen someone else's brand-new pocket calculator; the victim had complained to the principal. The principal had asked the teacher to conduct a surprise bag check.

Three teachers walked into our class and asked us all to put our bags up on the desk. Then they went to each bag, took every book out, held the bag upside down and shook it. Pages and pages of drawings depicting sexual acts in explicit detail tumbled out of my bag, fluttering to the ground like autumnal leaves.

My mother was called in. We sat together in the principal's office, she glaring at me as he laid the illustrations out on the table.

'What is this?' he asked.

'Michelangelo drew naked people,' I protested.

'Yes, but not doing it,' he replied.

My mother confiscated all my drawing pencils, took all my comic books and told me I wouldn't be allowed to close the door to my room until I was seventy years old. I was suspended from school for a week. At the end of that week, I was expelled.

There are details from this dark episode that still stab at me occasionally. Jagged shards of memory that poke through the haze of time and fill me with shame and regret. The staring, wide eyes of the girl seated two rows behind me as I was escorted out of the class by an astonished teacher clutching a bundle of pages. I had been planning to confess my feelings for this classmate that very day – I'd been working up the nerve to do so for months. The plan was to slip her a small note reading *I like you. Do you like me?* during recess. That note was lost in the cascade of incriminating pages.

I remember calling up one of my closest friends the day after and his mother answering the phone. 'He's not allowed to talk to you anymore. I don't think anyone should let their children talk to a pervert like you,' she said.

I remember my mother crying into the phone as she told my father what had happened. I even remember contemplating suicide. When you're thirteen and you find yourself without friends or even a school, the future seems quite bleak.

I didn't kill myself. I probably didn't even think about it more than once with any degree of seriousness. I don't think I even stopped masturbating for that long. Two months later, I was admitted into another school. I made new friends and collected new comics. It wasn't long before I had trained myself to forget the whole thing had happened.

The only real evidence of trauma showed itself when, a year after starting at the new school, the teachers announced a surprise bag check. Someone's brand-new pocket calculator had been stolen. (I suppose there was a massive underground black market for stolen pocket calculators in Karachi in the early 1990s.) The contents of my bag that day were nothing more than a few textbooks and probably a *Hardy Boys Casefiles,* but the moment it was my turn to hand the bag over to the teacher, I started shivering and sweating like a Vietnam War veteran suffering flashbacks while watching *Platoon.*

'Are you okay?' the teacher asked as she handed my bag back to me.

'Yes, miss,' I replied, then excused myself to go vomit in the toilet.

Years later, Pakistan was blessed with internet pornography. No more were our masturbatory needs limited by scarcity of supply. In the early days of dial-up connections, we used to have to sit and stare at a single picture loading slowly on a flickering monitor. Then video clips appeared online and internet speeds increased, so that the gap between clicking and relieving was minimal. People without internet access in their homes would go to cybercafés, gasping and sighing in the privacy of small booths fitted with all the necessities – computer, mouse, chair . . . and a box of tissues. It was a glorious time.

I once walked into a store near my house intending to buy a new horror movie DVD, and the man behind the counter nodded for me to come closer as he took the money.

'You look like the kind of man who watches porn,' he said with a salesman's grin.

When I got home I stared at my face in the mirror, trying to see what it was about my features that had tipped him off.

But then Pakistan changed again. In 2012, during a fit of religious cleansing, the government declared a ban on all porn sites. It was decided that internet pornography was ruining the 'youth of the nation'. Clearly, no one bothered to ask the 'youth of the nation' their opinion on all this. Soon, dedicated teams of cyber-censors catalogued and then blocked all the online smut. Pakistani males frantically scoured the web, hoping with each new browser refresh that they would be faced with a wall of questionable thumbnails and a gallery of sad people fornicating sadly, only to be met time and time again by the hateful THIS SITE IS RESTRICTED.

The effectiveness of the ban on online porn was enhanced by the hard work and dedication shown by a fifteen-year-old boy who gave the censors a list of over 780,000 websites that he claimed to have personally checked. For a fifteen-year-old to have done so without being reduced to a smouldering husk is, no doubt, some kind of epic feat that defies human physiology. Unfortunately, what he accomplished so proudly at fifteen, he no doubt came to regret deeply when he turned eighteen. History will remember him as one of the greatest villains mankind has ever known and only in his later years will he truly appreciate the damage that he wrought. Modern man is not equipped to deal with a world in which he has to make do with imagination alone. I tried. It was all in black and white.

Fortunately for me, I moved to Australia a few months after the ban took full effect. Sometimes I wonder if that was one of the motivations to get out of Pakistan. After all, with my personal history, whenever I masturbate to porn, I'm doing it to get revenge on society.

24

I was born a Pakistani. But it's never that simple – no one in Pakistan is just a Pakistani. Identities are divided and further subdivided by various classifications. First there is your geographic background, according to which you are either a Punjabi, a Sindhi, a Pathan, a Balochi or a Mohajir, that last being a name given to those who descended from people transplanted to Pakistan *after* its creation. Then there is your ethnic group; you are 'a Balochi from the Marri tribe' or 'a Sindhi from the Bhutto clan' or 'a Punjabi of Hyderabadi descent' and so on. Then there is your language and dialect: you could speak Sindhi or Pashto or Punjabi or Siraiki, or just Urdu, or even only English. Whatever remains of you is then carved up according to religious belief. It's never enough to be a Muslim; you have to be a certain kind of Muslim – a Sunni Barelvi, Sunni Hanafi, Shia Ashariya, Shia Bohra or Shia Ismaili. And this doesn't even take into account those unfortunate enough to not be born Muslim in a country that defines itself as an Islamic outpost. A miniscule percentage of a miniscule percentage of Pakistanis are Zoarastrian, Christian or Hindu. And beyond all of these, legally excluded from a right to existence, are the Ahmedis, a microscopic sect of Muslims who dare to challenge the finality of the prophethood in their own belief system and so have their persecution codified in the Pakistani constitution.

Thus I was born not just a Pakistani Muslim, but a Shia Ashariya Mohajir Karachiite who spoke English and Urdu. Almost all of those identifiers became problematic at some point, often individually and sometimes together.

The first time I experienced how the qualifiers of my existence changed perceptions was when I was six years old. Fahad, a school friend, had come over to play on the weekend and we had spent the entire Saturday morning fighting elaborate battles with our action figures. Around noon, my mother called us in for lunch: heaped plates of rice, daal and chicken qorma. Starved by the physical exertion of playing, I dug in. It was only when I had almost finished that I noticed my friend hadn't eaten any of his.

'Aren't you hungry?' I asked between mouthfuls.

'Yeah, but I can't eat this food,' said my friend.

'Why? Doesn't it taste good?'

'It's not that; it's because you're Shia. My mother said never to eat a Shia's food, because they spit in it before giving it to Sunnis.'

I considered this, then told him his mother was an idiot if she thought my mother spat in his food. We fought a bit, then went back to playing until his car came. That night, I asked my mother what a 'Shia' was.

'Where did you learn about Shias?' she asked.

'Fahad said we were Shias and that you spit in his food because he's a Sunil.'

'Sunni, not Sunil. And no, I didn't spit in his food. Who on earth told him that?'

'His mother.'

After muttering a few curse words – which, knowing her, were probably 'damned fool' and 'stupid woman' – my mother sat me down and explained the difference between a Shia and a Sunni. At the time I didn't understand most of the political intrigues and complex dynastic struggles involved in separating the two, so all that stuck with me was the Battle of Karbala.

I had heard about the battle of course. Every year, for the first ten days of the Islamic month of Muharram, my parents would attend large gatherings where the details of the battle would be narrated by an hysterically weeping imam. A stadium-sized car park would fill with cars, each containing families dressed entirely in black; we would sit in our cars listening to the narration over speakers that threatened to explode as the imam's voice reached operatic heights and then fell to a primal growl. Sitting in the back seat with my brother and sister, I'd listen to the story being told – of how the prophet's grandson, Hussein Ibn Ali, was trapped by his enemy, the treacherous Yazid, and, after several days of thirst and starvation, Hussein and his small caravan of supporters had been slaughtered. Our parents sniffled in the front at each telling. Afterwards, everyone in attendance would pat their chest in rhythmic unison, the more devout slapping their breasts so hard that the sound became like the repetitive cracking of a cannon.

On the tenth day, my father would take me to a parade where we would watch as people carried long poles crowned with symbols of Shia belief. Sometimes, if we stuck around long enough, I got to see the men who slashed their own backs with blades, swinging them from chains like nunchucks, while screaming, 'Ya Ali!' The grotesque morbidity of that expression of grief only struck me later in life – as a child I felt only awe.

My mother now explained to me how all these things were practices the Shias subscribed to and the Sunnis didn't. In her explanation it was implicitly conveyed that, by not doing so, the Sunnis were shirking a moral responsibility to honour the family of the very prophet they professed to love so much and, while they might not go to hell for this, they certainly were going to have to stand behind us Shias in the queue leading to heaven.

'You have to be careful, though,' my mother said, 'because there are more Sunnis than Shias.'

'So do we spit in their food?' I asked.

'No. That's just something stupid they all believe.'

'Do we believe anything like that about them?'

'No. We aren't stupid. Also, it's not right to judge someone by their religion. Your friend is still your friend. It doesn't matter if he is Sunni or Shia.'

It took me some time to understand what I had just learned, because it meant that my friends and I were now separated by beliefs we probably didn't fully comprehend, and by prejudices that were ridiculous and false but endorsed by adults. This wasn't helped by the fact that, a few days later, another boy at school said I was not to go near him because his grandmother had told him that Shias might kidnap him and kill him.

It also forced me to recalibrate my understanding of my parents, since, until then, I hadn't really considered them to be particularly religious. Religious people had beards, wore the hijab and threw spit-flecked Arabic inflections into words that have no use for them. My parents did none of that. That was when I first realised there were different categories of religious adherence. They are as follows:

GOOD MUSLIM: My parents are the perfect living example of this type of believer. They believe fervently in Allah, the Quran and the Prophet Muhammad. Both pray five times a day, give to the poor, have performed Hajj and end all praise with the grateful invocations of Allah's grace. Both my mother and father know certain passages of the Quran by heart, especially those that aid in searching for lost everyday items, and generally find pride in being a Muslim. My mother doesn't wear a hijab and my father doesn't have a beard. Nor do they think that the West was created by Satan and should be defeated in battle by inflicting maximum civilian casualties through random and creative acts of murderous suicide.

They do, however, think that America hates Muslims, that its support of Israel is evidence of this, further proven by the invasions of Afghanistan and Iraq. These are their opinions and, by and large, are no more toxic or damaging to the environment than my mother's belief that all men are inherently lazy and my father's belief that all women give terrible advice.

If you were to randomly select one hundred Muslims from around the world, chances are they would all be like my parents. Islam is a part of their life, but it doesn't get in the way.

BAD MUSLIM: Judged unfavourably by all other forms of Muslims, these are the second most common kind. They are Muslims by birth and by name. They may even go so far as to appreciate the sanctity of the Quran, Allah and his Prophet, but it ends there. They do not actually practise rituals and in general are reluctant even to publicly identify themselves as Muslim.

Some of them drink, despite the prohibitions, but none of them will ever eat pork. Pork is the final frontier for the Muslim. Sure, they may eye a strip of bacon lustfully if they ever encounter one, maybe even pause to consider a side of ribs after seeing it on a television show, but on average the safest place for a pig is in a Muslim country. For alcohol, though, there are all kinds of ready justifications provided. 'The Quran only outlaws a specific type of booze,' they say, pointing to the literal prohibition against wine made from fermented dates. Or, 'Islam is all about moderation,' they argue, just before passing out in a puddle of vodka and vomit.

In a Venn diagram of the beliefs shared between Good and Bad Muslims, the only overlap would be that Bad Muslims, too, think that America hates Muslims, that its support of Israel is evidence of this, further proven by the invasions of Afghanistan and Iraq.

TERRIBLE MUSLIM: Currently occupying every possible government job in any Muslim country you survey, another name for this breed of Muslim is 'Hypocritical Bastards'.

They are different from the Bad Muslims in that, while they may commit every sin and flout every prohibition, they present themselves as symbols of Islamic virtue. You can usually recognise them by the aggressively overt way they express their love for Islam. The men will have long, pious beards, with which they demonstrate both their commitment and masculinity; they have permanently bruised foreheads, to provide evidence of a lifetime spent prostrating on a prayer mat. Their women will wear the hijab – not wrapped tight, as is the custom, but instead floating several inches above an immense hairstyle that defies both the laws of physics and style.

They will always have in their hands a string of prayer beads on an endless rotation through busy fingers. Every prayer is read by both genders and every Hajj attended. Their commitment to the charade may even go so far as to see them shun alcohol and be completely loving and devoted husbands/wives. But put a rupee in front of them and they will serve up a round of bacon and ham while marrying a Kafir and swearing an oath to Satan.

They can also be counted in the club of people who believe that America hates Muslims, that its support of Israel is evidence of this, further proven by the invasions of Afghanistan and Iraq. The only difference here is that most of them tend to be quite willing to cosy up to their enemy if the price is right. Actually, that's not true. It's not if the price is right – it's if there is any price at all.

FRIGHTENING MUSLIM: Tends to talk about Jihad a lot. Your average mosque imam is a good example. In appearance the Frightening Muslim is not that different from the Terrible Muslim, only the FM has a greater commitment to the lifestyle. The men will not just sport beards but have shaved upper lips as well. This stylish look is rooted in the belief that the Prophet wore his beard in the same way, although there is no actual evidence to prove this. Nor is there any to prove that his pyjamas ended several inches above his ankles, but that is also a popular sartorial choice among this lot.

Now I should also provide some clarification about my introduction to this class of Muslim. The Frightening Muslim may say 'Jihad' a lot and talk about fighting the West and how the Muslim Ummah needs to rise up in revolt, but chances are you will never find one anywhere near a front line.

They are classified as Frightening, by the way, only by Westerners who see the stuff of terroristic nightmares in their appearance. For their fellow Muslims, this kind tends to be annoying at most and ridiculous at best. We tolerate them because on average they are useful in teaching your children the Quran (as long as you ensure that the education is limited to Arabic rote memorisation and does not include any kind of opinion-forming rhetoric or casual molestation). Their opinions range from far-fetched conspiracies – in which Islamic sects other than the one they belong to are plotting their downfall – to the belief that America hates Muslims, that its support of Israel is evidence of this, further proven by the invasions of Afghanistan and Iraq. An example of the Frightening Muslim is the entire country of Saudi Arabia.

DOWNRIGHT CRAZY MUSLIM: They believe that America hates Muslims, that its support of Israel is evidence of this, further proven by the invasions of Afghanistan and Iraq. What sets them apart from other Muslims is that they want to do something about it. And that something includes killing Westerners, killing active supporters of the West, killing passive supporters of the West, killing anyone who is in the way of getting to the actives, passives and Westerners, and, finally, just killing everyone. Examples of the Downright Crazy Muslim include Osama bin Laden, Ayman Al Zawahiri, all of Al-Qaeda and the Taliban.

--------- • ---------

A year after I first encountered the concept of religious difference, my mother hired a man to teach me the Quran, the learning of which is a duty every Muslim must fulfil, even if it's taught entirely in Arabic and is thus completely incomprehensible. The mullah would come to our house and spend an hour trying to get me to read it. I say 'trying' because the one thing that no one can do with complete success is get a seven-year-old boy to read Arabic that he doesn't even understand for more than thirty seconds at a time. Our sessions were thus punctuated by escape attempts, feigned illness, skipped pages and countless other attempts to slow down an already laborious process.

The first mullah I had was an ancient man with an immense beard that had been dyed orange, so it looked like his chin was on fire. He had neither the energy nor the patience to match me, and after a year he gave up the fight and resigned. The next one was younger, with a beard that was still naturally black and the energy to attempt to overcome my limited attention span. On Monday, Wednesday and Friday, from 3 pm to 4 pm, he would sit with me at the dining table and listen to me recite ancient Arabic verses. I would read aloud, my diction a series of spastic bursts of unintelligible phlegm-rattling sounds as I did my best to imitate what I thought Arabic sounded like.

Maybe it would have been easier had I known what exactly I was reading. But, other than sharing the same script and rules of grammar as my native Urdu, Arabic was completely alien to me. Nor was I unique in this linguistic failing. It's safe to say that the majority of Pakistanis can read Arabic at the same level of fluency that they can read Urdu, but almost none of them would understand the meaning of the words they read. Unfortunately, no one bothered to tell me that I was not alone in my ignorance and so the entire experience of reading the Quran was one that filled me with frustration and anxiety.

Under the new mullah's stern guidance (I never got to know any of their names, they were always just 'Maulvi Sahib'), over the next three years I slowly worked my way through almost all 114 chapters. I would have completed it under his tutelage, if he hadn't decided to try molesting me.

I'm not sure why he chose to wait until I was ten before he attempted to jumpstart my sexual awakening. I don't think I was particularly fetching at that age, definitely not any more than I had been the year before or even three years before. Maybe he had been working his way around the bases, as they say, but in such a subtle manner that I hadn't noticed. Or maybe it was just that, on this particular day, the sexual frustration which dogs every Pakistani male happened to overtake his judgment.

Either way, one afternoon, as I sat there stopping and starting my way through another sentence written in calligraphic Arabic script, my ears red hot with annoyance, Maulvi Sahib told me to sit on his lap. I'm sure at the time it must have seemed like an odd request, and I probably hesitated for a few seconds before agreeing to do so, But he was an Adult and generally you were supposed to do what Adults said. That was why you sat in the back seat of the car, when obviously you wanted to sit in the front; it was why you didn't eat dessert for lunch and you didn't wear your underwear over your pants, at least in public. Adults told you what you should and shouldn't do and obedient children followed these rules, well, obediently.

So, pulling my copy of the Quran across the table, I sat on his lap and continued to read. It wasn't long, however, before I began to feel an uncomfortable nudging against my bum. His arms were resting on the table, bracketing me in, and his legs were clearly both in place, stretched out between my knees. Quick maths led me to the obvious conclusion that the increasingly persistent poke I felt against my bottom wasn't from any of his limbs. I also noticed that he had begun to gently rock back and forth, with my scrawny body echoing his steady momentum.

Now, faced with such a situation, a ten-year-old boy has several options:

Option A: Run.

Option B: Confront.

Option C: Sit awkwardly and silently until everything is over, and then go tell your parents.

Option D: Sit awkwardly and silently until everything is over and then never tell anyone, instead choosing to bury the trauma in a pillow full of screams and a lifetime of sexual confusion.

Option E: Fight.

I chose Option E. Actually, I chose a combination of Options A, C and E.

First, I swung around in his lap and punched him in the face. That was the intent anyway. Being an uncoordinated boy who was basically being dry-humped, my aim was a little off. The bony fist I unleashed, with all my fury and confusion, missed his face entirely. It did, however, find a point of contact on his throat. He let out a surprised yelp that turned into a gagging cough. His hands clawed wildly at me, but a second too late. The element of surprise was on my side so, before he could grab hold of me, I was bolting out of the room, up the stairs and headlong into my parents' room.

My father was away on the ship, but my mother was very much at home. Her annoyance at her gasping and spluttering son, who had crashed into the side of her bed, turned to concern when she noticed I was crying, and then to rage when I managed to explain what had happened. Although how she managed to understand anything, given that all I could emit was a continuous high-pitched scream, is beyond me.

My mother shot out of the room like an immense maternal bullet. As she half-ran, half-leaped down the stairs with surprising agility, she called out for help from my father's brother, who was working on the other side of the house. She reached the landing just as he emerged from his room, panicked by her screams.

The mullah had, by this time, made a run for it. I imagine it wasn't easy, with his throat constricted and his erection swinging recklessly in his pyjamas, but he somehow made it out of the house and to his motorcycle before my mother and uncle caught up with him. We never saw him again.

Once my mother had caught her breath, she had a lengthy talk with me about how I should always tell her if anyone ever touched me in an inappropriate way. I promised to do so, even though I didn't a year later when a shopkeeper, after taking the money I was paying for a textbook, reached down and squeezed my genitals. That molestation was so sudden and brief that it barely registered at the time.

I did finally complain to my mother about an aunt from my father's side who had a peculiar penchant for lightly spanking me whenever I was within striking distance. But she was senile and my mother wasn't sure what advice to give other than: 'Just stay out of her reach.'

By then I had convinced myself it was just how people must have shown affection for children in her time.

Years later, I was sitting with several friends and the conversation shifted to molestation experiences. We were unsurprised to discover that of the fifteen boys and girls sitting together, all of us had been molested at some point in our childhoods, many more than once. Over the years, further informal surveys have only confirmed this. I don't know how commonly children are used for sexual gratification in other countries, but the casualness with which it occurs in places like Pakistan was horrific to me, especially when I became the parent of a child myself.

I eventually finished the Quran a year later, an event celebrated with cake and cash rewards. My third, and finally successful, instructor was a diminutive and soft-spoken old lady who was awarded the honour of teaching my sister and brother as well. Since she was barely capable of staying awake, unless plied with cup after cup of tea, she seemed unlikely to be able to work up the energy required to molest someone.

--------- • ---------

Other than the sermons attended during Muharram, Quran classes and the Islamic Studies class at school, religion was fairly irrelevant to our lives. By ninth grade I had three close friends of whom two were Sunni and the other Shia, but we were too caught up in girls, comics and the impending Cambridge-administered O-level exams to care about what kind of Muslim we were.

Teimoor's family had moved into the rented half of our house around that time and, being of the same age with identical interests, we became best friends. His father was Shia and his mother was Sunni, but since his father had walked out on the family, he was brought up marginally Sunni and with no real interest in any of it. His bedroom was right next to mine; although our parents prohibited us from talking (because we were both doing poorly in our studies and spending all our time creating comics instead), he would swing across from his balcony onto my window ledge and we would continue our conversations there.

Ahsan came from a more traditional Sunni family and even had a brief phase of intense religiosity shortly after we became friends, but his approach to Islam was more focused on the Sufi spiritual traditions.

And finally there was Sajjad, who was more aggressively Shia than his parents ever were; his passion for our minority belief was fuelled by the increasing killings of Shias in Pakistan. Convinced that the only way to combat anti-Shia terrorism was by putting up a poster of Ayatollah Khomeini in his bedroom, he became fluent in all aspects of Shia Islam. His fervency was, of course, tempered by his love of Jon Secada songs and our shared passion for Junoon's albums.

By then I had already begun flirting with atheism, mostly out of the realisation that I was only a Muslim because I was born one. This epiphany was a result of the Islamic Studies teacher at school asking us one day what exactly made us Muslims and not, say, Christians. He was hoping for a listing of the various differences in belief and practice; instead, I raised my hand and said, 'It's because we were born Muslims, sir. If we were born into a Christian family, we'd be Christian, right?'

These days, a child voicing such controversial common sense would be branded a blasphemer and probably beaten to death in the streets. It has happened plenty of times in Pakistan in the last decade. But back then, my teacher was calm enough to smile, say I made a good point and then ask me to list Muslim beliefs and practices. Years later,

I heard he had left Pakistan because students in another school in Karachi were offended by his tolerance for debating the intellectual requirements of belief and had accused him of blasphemy. Facing death, he was forced to flee his homeland.

The distinction between Shias and Sunnis and the various other forms of Islam actually became fairly taboo topics in school because of the increasing violence between those groups in the outside world. Shias were being killed across Pakistan, their very existence deemed an act of blasphemy by the growing extremist groups that had begun taking root in the country. Gunmen raided mosques, shooting down people as they prayed; bombs were thrown into schools run by Shia charity groups; and Shia professionals – doctors, airline pilots and judges – were shot at by terrorists on motorcycles. While the police and the government weren't advocating such murders, their inability to stop them was its own form of encouragement.

'If anyone asks you if you are a Shia or a Sunni,' my mother told me in those days, 'tell them you're a Muslim.'

Every Muharram, I would get plugged into the Shia community, the ritual events of the first ten days becoming my only real religious commitments. We attended the narrative sermons, walked the procession and wore black.

But security increased every year, with armed guards protecting entrance and exit routes, and cars regularly checked for attackers. It was in reaction to this growing tension that my friend Sajjad became increasingly religious, embracing his Shia beliefs with overt pride. Even I, with my growing atheism, found an affinity with Shi'ism. For me, it wasn't about the religious connotations that came with being a Shia but connecting to the cultural heritage. I was part of a minority that had been persecuted throughout history and whose very origins came from a tale of persecution that had occurred more than a thousand years before.

The passion demonstrated each year during the retelling of the Battle of Karbala is often mocked by outsiders, who fail to understand that it isn't just literal grief over the martyrdom of a spiritual leader – it's a metaphor for never surrendering to oppression. Shias carry the burden of sacrificial martyrdom with them everywhere, on a daily basis. I felt a powerful resonance with that cultural connection and found myself unable to shift it as easily as I had been able to shrug off religious belief. I was probably the world's first Shia atheist. A minority within a minority within a minority.

When I went to college in America, I met Jewish people for the first time – Israelis and American Jews who, until then, I only knew of from political discussions in Pakistan about the persecution of the Palestinians. I knew I vehemently disagreed with the way Israel was treating Palestinians, but I became close friends with some Jews and actually found myself relating to their particular sense of humour.

The Jewish identity is famously built on a history of persecution met with defiance. It's much the same for the Shias of the world. A reviewer once described my comedy persona as a 'Pakistani Woody Allen'. While I think that's too high praise to be accurate and was probably referring more to my physical appearance, I'm sure many Jewish comedians would identify with the confusion of self-deprecation and nervous confidence inherent in my approach to the world. If Israel and Iran found a way to get along, they'd be surprised at how much they made each other laugh.

25

I barely survived my O-levels; putting my head down at the absolute last minute, I studied just enough to pass. My parents were thrilled that I had passed but disappointed that I had not passed with better grades, although by now they had grown used to the taste of disappointment.

That Teimoor, Ahsan and Sajjad had all done significantly better than me made it that much worse. Parents love using the analogy 'If your friends jumped in a lake, would you?' to dissuade you from doing anything rebellious, but they find conformity more attractive when it comes to studying. That I had studied for the O-levels during continuously rolling power outages and taken the exams under threat of death was not taken into consideration, because so had everyone else.

For the latter part of the 1990s, Pakistan's democratically elected governments waged war on Karachi. The city made too much money and was too individualistic for them not to covet it. But control of Karachi's coffers lay in the hands of a political party that claimed to represent Mohajir rights while operating as a criminal empire. The government's attempts to dislodge the city's powerbrokers was a bloody and violent enterprise that eventually failed, but not before the streets had been littered with bodies. Mohajir groups and government forces fought gun battles in the open, shutting the entire city down for several days at a time. Rumours circulated of torture cells discovered in residential neighbourhoods and gunny sacks packed with body parts found on roadsides, with blame for these falling on both sides.

'If anyone asks if you're a Mohajir,' my father told me in those days, 'tell them you're a Pakistani.'

The violence was accompanied by a growing power crisis – electricity shortages plunged the city into darkness on a daily basis. We studied for the exams sitting on rooftops, desperate for evening breezes, our books illuminated by candles and battery-powered torches. Some of it was bound to take a toll on my focus – although, to be perfectly honest, it was mostly that instead of studying I spent my time reading, drawing comic books and masturbating.

Fortunately, my grades were not so low as to prevent me from gaining admission to one of the better A-level institutes in Karachi. The Lyceum was housed in a building so small that the word 'Institute' is probably bigger than the plot of land on which it sat. Most of the other students were just like me: kids who had got grades that were neither great nor terrible. Together, the eighty or so boys and girls who happily crowded those tiny classes were the epitome of adequacy. According to the Cambridge educational system, we had lifetimes of middling achievement to look forward to, never rising above nor sinking below.

This vision of our futures didn't have the effect I assume the educators desired. It certainly didn't make us rise to the challenge, declaring, 'We'll show you!' Instead, the responsibility of achievement was entirely lifted from our shoulders, giving us even more time to devote to plotting how best to wrap ourselves around the opposite sexes.

I'd always thought that, if only we had been allowed to have one great orgy on the first day of school, with everyone going at it hammer and tongs with anyone in their line of sight, then tension would have been relieved and we could have gone on to become productive members of society. But authority has always been prudish, and so no orgies were authorised. Instead, we threw ourselves into the awkward rituals of courting.

This was an activity we had a great deal of time for, given that studying is purely incidental during A-levels, at least for the first year and a half. Almost everyone who had survived the previous O-level exams realised that the years we spent in frightful preparation had been wasted time. To truly do well, all you needed to do was spend the three months prior to the exams shovelling information into your brain, with no regard for analysis.

Conversations on the first day of A-levels were usually along the lines of 'Which school did you come from?' and 'What subjects are you taking?' so we would know how to classify each other. Every private school in Karachi is associated with generalisations of some sort, true or not. School A is a middle-class boys' school, so everyone who went there could be classified as frustrated and violent. School B is a co-ed school with rich kids, so everyone is pampered and liberal. And so on. That being said, there was one characteristic shared by all the students. A-levels in Pakistan is how I imagine first-year college is in America: classes are incidental, studying accidental. Mostly, it is about dating and learning how to go to parties.

Of course, I stayed single for the entire time, though not by choice. There were many girls I would have happily stuck to like a remora on a shark's back, but I lacked the confidence required to ask them out. And they lacked the vision to see that the skinny boy with thick spectacles and a terrible haircut was also deeply romantic, and probably an incredible kisser. A-levels is also when I first met Ishma. A year ahead of me, she was directing a play for which I auditioned. I instantly developed a slightly creepy habit of peeking at her out of the corner of my eye and stalking her from a distance. (Now, of course, she claims that she was also attracted to me back then and wished I would ask her out. I think it's a lie she tells herself to justify the grievous misstep in taste and common sense she committed by marrying me years later.) The two years of A-levels were spent, then, in longing.

Meanwhile, Karachi's violence had achieved a kind of monotonous regularity, as had the entire nation's political uncertainty. Democratic governments usurped other democratic governments and the gunfire faded into background noise. Political awareness flared up briefly during the nuclear tests of 1998 and then I left for America, hoping I was leaving all the distillations of my identity behind.

26

Karachi changed when I became a father. From 2003 to 2009, the violence increased by fits and blasts, but it never occurred to me that I needed to escape it. Ishma first broached the prospect of immigration in 2007 after returning from Melbourne, where she had just spent a year studying. Melbourne was ranked as one of the top-five cities in the world in which to live by one of those lists that comes out every few months; Karachi was right near the bottom.

Despite her rational arguments for why we should try to leave the latter for the former, I talked her out of it by reminding her that, even though the city was dangerous, our lives were comfortable. We lived at home with my parents; we had jobs we both loved; we had family who needed us as much as we needed them and a close group of friends. That many of these friends had already started to move away seemed like an unnecessarily hysterical response to me. But I had just started work at Dawn News and my stand-up comedy shows were growing in popularity.

Ishma didn't see it that way, having just experienced the independence that Australia offers a woman. There she could walk anywhere she wanted without fear of molestation, could dress however she wanted without fear of condemnation. I didn't understand at first how intoxicating those freedoms were for her, and how returning to Karachi made her yearn for them more than she had ever done before.

All that changed the day Anya was born. Seeing the world as being full of danger and threat is a fairly typical response to becoming a parent. When politicians try to justify such policies as increased surveillance, intrusive security measures or ethnic and religious screening by using the argument 'How would you react if it was your child at risk?', they are being disingenuous. If I had to decide on how the world should be, and my only consideration was that my daughter needed to be safe, then everyone dies. I would kill everybody – furniture designers who make tables with sharp edges, plastic-bag manufacturers . . . and basically every male over the age of six.

Seeing nothing but hazards and potential death everywhere is the only appropriate response to being given charge of a tiny, defenceless baby. This was exacerbated by the fact that we lived in a city where the highest degree of paranoid panic was justified. Every time we went anywhere in the car, I worried about a stray bullet hitting her, a bomb blast going off too close or kidnappers targeting her.

Children are abducted, raped and killed with such regularity in Pakistan that it hardly even gets noticed anymore. The newspapers publish stories about little girls found dead all the time and I had barely even read the headlines of those articles when I was doing my daily scour for newsworthy stories as a producer. But when I became a father, they were all I could see. Every day another infant's body was found in Karachi. Every day brought a new story about a child being raped. I read them all, obsessing over how powerless I was to prevent such things from happening. In a city where such things occurred so often, I believed it was only a matter of time before it was our turn.

Panic began to take over my life. I couldn't work, couldn't read, couldn't even carry a conversation without visualising Anya kidnapped, crying for her parents, and us unable to reach her. So I looked for a way out. By then we had heard stories from friends in Canada about how the job market there was abysmal. England had begun tightening its immigration laws, squeezing out anyone from Pakistan in particular. Emigrating to America wasn't possible without a job offer already in place. Australia became the only viable option; a lawyer told us that, with Ishma's psychology degree, we would get work visas there in no time. We paid him a large portion of our savings and waited for our exit ticket. It came three years later.

Australian immigration works at a glacial pace, which is slowed even further when the applicants are from high-risk countries like Pakistan. For those three years, we put our lives on hold. We stuck with the jobs we had, avoided making any major investments and saved every single rupee we earned towards the migration we kept hoping was just around the corner.

In the meantime, I learned to suppress my constant anxiety to a manageable background migraine-level. It would flare up every few months, exhibiting itself as a crippling stomach cramp, blinding headache or peculiar skin rash. I was writing the weekly newspaper columns by then and the research they required was making plain to me the direction in which Pakistan seemed to be headed. Religious extremism was rising, not just in the terrorist groups that were waging war on the civilian population, but among ordinary people as well.

In May 2010, a mosque full of Ahmedi worshippers was attacked by terrorists. They killed ninety-four innocent people who had simply been offering their Friday prayer. No one condemned the attack at an official level. Even people in my office justified it by arguing that

Ahmedis committed blasphemy by their very existence, and so their deaths were justified.

In January 2011, the governor of Punjab, Salmaan Taseer, was assassinated. His mistake had been to champion the cause of a Christian woman falsely accused of blasphemy who, under Pakistani laws, would be condemned to death for her supposed crime. For daring to criticise the blasphemy law, he was killed by his own security guard. Instead of mourning his murder, many in the country celebrated it. His killer was showered with rose petals and educated people across the country said the governor had deserved to die.

Four months later, Shahbaz Bhatti, the only Christian federal minister in the country, was murdered for daring to demand more protection for minorities. His death too went unmourned and unavenged.

More Shias were killed, often massacred in large numbers, with no one rising to their defence. In Quetta, buses were regularly stopped by armed extremists and the Shia passengers forced to disembark; after being identified, they were then murdered. Ahmedis were shot on a near-daily basis, their killings even advocated on national television by religious scholars. Most of these murders went undocumented in the mainstream news, and those responsible were blatantly protected by the government and military. Any attempt to draw attention to them was deemed unpatriotic; the country was growing increasingly obsessed with its national image and national character, treating any criticisms levelled against it as an attempt to undermine those nebulous qualities.

I wrote articles about all of this and each one resulted in a furious barrage of death threats. These threats weren't coming from terrorist groups – Al-Qaeda and the Taliban weren't penning poorly spelled responses to my 600-word pleas for sanity – but from people with the same educational and financial background as me. For daring to discuss how we were becoming much like, as I saw it, pre-World War II Nazi Germany, I was called a traitor, an American spy and anti-Islamic.

A new phrase entered the vernacular: Liberal Fascist. If you dared to preach secularism and equal human rights for religious minorities and women, then you were a 'Liberal Fascist', intent on destroying our proudly Islamic nation. Major political parties were becoming overtly sympathetic towards extremist ideology and those that weren't were targeted with violence until their voices were muted. Friends whom I had always considered politically aware and intelligent showed shocking ignorance of the constant oppression so many of our fellow citizens were subjected to on a daily basis; even some members of my extended family began placing greater value on patriotic rhetoric than the protection of anyone who wasn't a Sunni male.

During the application process for the Australian visa, we were required to get police clearance certificates for ourselves, to prove that we hadn't ever been convicted of any crimes. The paperwork usually takes a week or so, but ours had been held up by the neighbourhood police station for a month. I went there to demand an explanation for the delay, expecting the fault to lie in bureaucratic laziness or ineptitude. Instead, the officer responsible for clearing the paperwork showed me two stacks of police clearance requests, each one taller than I was.

'These are all from Hindus and Christians,' he told me. 'Everyone who can is leaving the country. I grew up with Hindu and Christian friends. My superintendent was a Hindu. Now, they are all going. Pakistan is not safe for any of them anymore. I'm not Hindu or Christian, but if I could, I would go too.'

A few months later, I was asked to submit our passports. Anya hadn't travelled abroad yet and so I needed to acquire one for her. Pakistan is the only country which, when issuing a passport, requires its citizens to sign a statement declaring Ahmedis as non-Muslims, thus making everyone in the country complicit in their persecution. When confronted with the document for signing, I refused.

I expected a fight, maybe to be arrested or beaten. Instead, the man responsible for the paperwork said he'd skip over that portion for a bribe. Corruption is the only thing that still overrules religious fanaticism.

27

In February 2012, our lawyer called to tell us we had finally received our Australian visas. We decided that we still needed a few months to maximize our savings and organise our lives before we left and so set our deadline as the first week of June. I told the advertising company I'd be wrapping up in a few weeks and did a few final stand-up shows to earn some extra money.

As the deadline drew nearer, we began to have the predictable misgivings. What if we were just overreacting? Many others were staying in Karachi and it's not like we had been killed yet. What if we went to Australia and there were no jobs and we came back six months later with our savings spent and had to pick up exactly where we had left off? Australia was too far away. How could Anya grow up without her grandparents around all the time? How would we survive without our friends? Karachi, fortunately, had a way of reminding us of why we had begun this process.

Everyone gets held up at gunpoint in Karachi. I know people who have even been robbed two or three times in the same month. It's so common that, if you haven't ever been robbed, it's probably because you're the one holding the gun. Karachiites don't even react to it anymore, referring to it as just another tax that they have to pay. The procedure is always the same: at a traffic light, a motorcyclist will hold a gun to your head, you will give up your phone, wallet and any other valuables he asks for, then he will leave with them. If you argue, delay in any way or are simply too slow to respond, you get shot.

A Dawn News cameraman was relieved of his camera equipment by a thief who shot a pedestrian walking past just to show he was serious. My father and sister were robbed once while sitting in the car outside a shop waiting for me to buy chocolate. In the time it took for me to pick up a Snickers bar and pay, they had been relieved of their phones at gunpoint.

My turn came just a few weeks before we were scheduled to leave for Australia. I was driving home from work, lurching my way through rush-hour traffic. There is an intersection less than two minutes from my house and I was stuck there, waiting for the light to turn green, with the windows rolled down, because the air conditioner in the car had committed honourable suicide after failing to combat the summer heat. I was singing along to some classic rock song, my earbuds leading to the phone nestled under my crotch. I didn't notice the man until he put a gun to my temple: 'Phone and wallet.'

I observed the protocol, quickly pulling out my phone and wallet and handing them over. Then, for reasons I still don't understand, he smiled.

'I hope you aren't angry with me,' he said.

And for reasons I also still don't understand, I replied, 'You've taken my phone and my wallet, at least leave me my anger.'

I remember flinching the moment I said it, expecting him to shoot me for my flippant response. Instead, he burst out laughing.

I think I surprised him. Comedy does that – it's all about catching you unawares. Kind of like crime. And because he laughed, I laughed. Before he went quiet.

The gun was still pressed to the side of my head this entire time. But then he stuffed it into the waistband of his jeans, pulled his shirt over it, and gave me back my phone and wallet.

I stared at him in confusion. 'I . . . I don't understand,' I said.

He reached in and patted my head. 'I have to do this,' he said. 'If I don't, I get killed. It's the only way I can feed my family and the families of all my friends who have been killed. But you are a good person, I can see that. I'm not going to do this to a good person. That would be wrong.'

Then he walked away. I sat there in silence, staring at my phone and wallet until the light turned green and the car behind me began blaring its horn.

I have a theory about what happened. I think that, because I made him laugh, for a brief moment we connected on a human level. Shared laughter broke through the facade that had been created. I wasn't the victim anymore and he wasn't the thief. We were just two people laughing at a joke, and that made him see me as human and made him see himself as human too. And, briefly, that shared humanity overrode the roles that a violent society had prescribed for us. Either that or he was a terrible judge of character.

I was grateful. But I wasn't going to stick around long enough for that theory to be tested again.

28

It's the rituals and traditions we accumulate around ourselves that are the hardest to let go. I still find it next to impossible to go to the toilet without a comic book in hand, for example. And when those rituals involve other people, the bond that is then created between the adherents is nearly impossible to break.

Teimoor, Ahsan, Sajjad and I had been friends since ninth grade. Over the years, others had drifted into the group, some remaining and some drifting away again. But at the core remained the four of us. Together we had collected comics, played Dungeons & Dragons, discovered porn, suffered through each other's bouts of heartbreak and even counselled one another through personal traumas. When we met the women we would each marry, it was important that those women respect the depths of our friendship, even if they found it a bit amusing.

The central ritual around which our bond had been forged was not – as we kind of, sort of wished it had been – surviving a great battle together; nor had it been holding on to each other as we tumbled off a great cliff, with one man's grip on an outcrop the only thing between us and death. It was far more mundane, yet just as important: every evening we had tea together. We all lived within a mile of one another and smack in the centre of the routes between each other's homes was a small tea cafe.

To call it a cafe is probably giving it a great deal more credit than it deserved. It was a small shop with tables and chairs arranged on the dirty footpath in front. The rest of the patrons were mostly rickshaw drivers, taxi drivers and other shopkeepers, which meant the tea was excellent: stiff as a starched shirt and brewed until it smelled of colonial ghosts. From grade nine to the end of our A-levels we sat there every day, on creaking plastic furniture, with street cats prowling around our table for scraps of naan, talking over tea. Some of the most important issues of our lives were dissected at those evening tea sessions, although most of the time the conversation was about whether or not Hulk was stronger than Thor.

The tea sessions were interrupted when we dispersed for college, Ahsan travelling to Lahore, Sajjad to Canada and I to America. Left in Karachi, Teimoor went there for tea on his own some days and was once spotted by Sajjad's mother. Her description of our friend sitting alone at a table with three empty chairs around him almost broke our collective hearts, and we were glad to resume the ritual when we all returned to Pakistan once our higher education was complete.

As we got jobs, then got married, the daily tea became weekly, then monthly, then maybe just a couple of times a year. Teimoor was the first to leave Karachi again, migrating to London with his wife. Sajjad got married and left for Jeddah a year or so later and by then Ahsan and his wife had moved to a distant part of the city. I drove past the cafe every now and then, mostly on my way to somewhere else, and sometimes I'd see other groups of boys sitting there and laughing over their own cups. When I'd tell Ahsan about it, we'd make plans to return together, but never really got around to it.

Until, that is, the night I was leaving for Australia. That evening, Ahsan came over and we drove down to the cafe one last time. We sat at the same table, were attended by what were probably the same grizzled cats, and sipped the same cups of tea we had done for so many years. Two chairs sat empty next to us and we took pictures of them and sent them off to Sajjad and Teimoor. To our dismay, the street was much filthier than we remembered and we spent most of the time trying to keep flies from kamikaze diving into the tea. The cats were more aggressive, bordering on intimidating, and even the old waiters who used to know us by name were no longer there. Only the tea still tasted good. We drank it, then Ahsan dropped me back home.

A few hours later, after our parents were done crying, Ishma, Anya and I left Karachi.

I, NORTHAM

29

We flew to Australia with a plan. We needed a plan, because immigration is too frightening without one. To leave the country in which we grew up – where we had spent almost our entire lives, had lifelong friends, successful careers, knew the customs and traditions and cultural expectations – and then to aim ourselves at a place that was utterly alien filled us with terror. .

In the weeks leading up to our departure, I had severe abdominal cramps; my stomach bloated to twice its normal size. I was taken to the hospital and a doctor gave me a painkiller and told me to stop stressing so much and, no, I didn't have stomach cancer – I was just pregnant with farts.

Ishma handled her panic by focusing her attention on the task of packing our belongings and sorting out what we would take with us and what we would leave behind. Geographically neutral clothes, like jeans and t-shirts – take. Culturally specific clothes, like shalwar kameezes and sherwanis – leave. Computers, phones and peripheral technology – take. Books – leave. That was the most difficult decision. Between us we had a sizeable library of autographed hardcovers, ragged softcovers and a few thousand comics and graphic novels. Shipping them to Australia would cost too much, and carrying them around until we found a place to settle would be an unnecessary burden. She packed them all with an archaeologist's care so that when we eventually sent for them, they would still be as we'd left them.

Anya, of course, was just three years old and so too young to comprehend that we were leaving her grandparents and her first home and moving to an entirely different continent. We made every effort to keep our anxiety hidden from her, but children are rogue radars, plucking emotional frequencies from the air, regardless of your best intentions. She became more clingy and desperate for attention, traits an only child surrounded by adoring grandparents can have in limitless quantities. Our parents did as parents do, indulging her so much that she developed early-onset megalomania and then sighing mournfully every time they looked at us.

'Creating a Plan' was, for us, liking building a wall to block out the zombies that kept assaulting us with their moans of 'noooo jooooob' and 'maaaaking a biiiig mistaaaake'. The plan was: We land in Perth, spend at most two days with Ishma's cousin, who had been living there for almost a decade, rent a house in Mandurah – a city half an hour's drive from Perth – and then begin the job search. If in three months we haven't found any jobs, we head back to Karachi and pretend like the whole thing never happened. Not the best of plans, but it's what we came up with.

The reason we were landing in Perth and moving to Mandurah was because of the visa our lawyer had got for us. He kept the details of the visa secret until our passports had been returned with stamped invitations from the Australian embassy, thus guaranteeing he received his contractual payment. The visa, it turned out, didn't let us just move to Melbourne as we had hoped. Instead, Australia's Department of Immigration had confined us to regional Western Australia, where we had to spend two years living and working before being allowed access to the rest of the country. Even Perth, the largest city in the state, was forbidden to us.

I spent the months between the lawyer's shock announcement and our departure researching our options. According to Wikipedia, of all the remote town and cities that make up regional WA, the one most likely to provide us with employment and access to the comforts of a modern urban environment was Mandurah – almost a million people living close enough to Perth that it served as an extended suburb to the larger city. So that's where we put the proverbial pin in our map and decided we would wait out the two-year sentence.

There are important lessons I've learned about immigration because of those first few days. Lessons worth imparting to other hopeful migrants:

- No matter how much money you bring with you, it's never enough.
- Without friends or family already in the city and willing to commit acts of charity on your behalf, it's almost impossible.
- And, most importantly, plans are completely bloody useless.

Instead of two days, we stayed with Ishma's cousin for two weeks, and instead of moving to the bustling city of Mandurah, we ended up in the small farming town of Northam.

Ishma's cousin, Mehreen, had spent a significant portion of her life in Australia, her parents having migrated there decades before. She lived close to the centre of the city with her husband, Ali, and their two sons. That both boys were close to Anya's age relieved us of the burden of distracting her. When we arrived, Ali and Mehreen listened to our plan, laughed until they could barely breathe and then told us to unpack our suitcases because we weren't going to move anywhere for the next few weeks.

'No one finds a job in just a few days,' Ali told us, 'and you'll use up all your savings in two months if you move to Mandurah.'

He was right, of course. We needed a car right away; he saved me the search by selling me an old car parked in his driveway that had been used by visiting relatives. This was the car that I eventually sacrificed to the Kangaroo Gods that watch over Australia's highways. He also edited Ishma's résumé, prioritising the parts that would appeal to Australian recruiters, and he showed us how to find jobs advertised online.

Mehreen showed us where to shop and what to buy, saving us from overspending on essentials like winter clothing and linens; she gave me my first lessons in cooking. We settled into their house, taking grateful advantage of their endless hospitality and experience, and then we began to panic about the absence of a new plan.

Perth reminds me of the parts of Northern Virginia that lie just outside Washington DC. A cluster of high-rise office towers and hipster bars are squeezed inside the CBD, surrounded by a galaxy of generic suburbs, most of which are connected to the centre by wide highways. As you rocket along them, it's hard to believe how spread out the whole place is, especially when its entire population is equal to the attendance at a Karachi wedding. It is a city not yet fully convinced that it wants to be a city.

Because of Australia's upside-down weather, we flew out of a sweat-sodden Karachi summer right into one of the coldest winters Western Australia had ever experienced. Anya and I immediately fell ill, wheezing when our scrawny lungs were touched by the lightest chill. Ishma luxuriated in the freedom on offer by jogging through the streets every morning and walking everywhere, while I burrowed under several layers of sweaters and jackets.

Three days after we landed, we took Anya to Perth Zoo, something I had promised her we would do. There is a zoo in Karachi, but my memory of visiting it as a child was a deeply traumatic one – a bear with one eye and a lion so sickly and starved its mane had moulted, and every time it roared it sounded like a call for help. I had never gone back and was discouraged from even considering it after a friend told me he saw people feeding the monkeys crushed glass on a recent trip.

Like all little children, Anya loves animals and yearned to see something other than the goats and cows she got to briefly squeal over before their ritualistic sacrifice on Eid in Karachi. So the three of us spent a full day with our noses pressed against the glass enclosures at the Perth Zoo. Seeing Anya thrill over a family of orangutans made us confident that we had done the right thing.

Still, as our second week in Perth dawned and no job offers came in response to the applications we sent out every day, my anxiety began clawing back up. It was mostly in a bid to distract myself that I did a Google search for comedy clubs in Perth one evening. It turned out that Perth had a fairly vibrant stand-up comedy culture, with several venues hosting regular comedy nights during the week. I found out that there was actually one right up the street, with a show starting in a couple of hours, so I drove there to see what it was like.

It struck me that I had never been inside an actual comedy club, despite having been a stand-up comedian for several years at that point. The closest I'd come had been the virtual clubs in Second Life, and I doubted those were comparable. At the very least, actual comedy clubs were unlikely to be underwater and populated with sexualised wildlife in spikes and leather.

Lazy Susan's is a small fifty-seater comedy room above an expensive bar. The bar is full of men and women dressed in designer clothing; the men flaunt arms muscled like hydraulic pistons and the women bare several acres of combined cleavage. The comedy club upstairs, however, is full of hardcore comedy fans, with lots of ironic t-shirts and shrink-wrapped red jeans. All the men have beards that, when paired with their white skin, means they probably own several ukuleles and at least one banjo each. If I had a beard that unruly I'd be getting finger-banged at the airport. The women all watch animé, collect comics and have their hair dyed in several colours simultaneously – none of those colours can be found anywhere near the natural spectrum.

The club has inclined rows of chairs facing the small stage with an exposed brick wall behind it. During shows, the room is dark, with a single spotlight centred on the comedian on stage. The audience is small enough and pressed close enough for the comedy to feel intimate and the laughter shared. It's exactly how I always wanted a comedy club to be.

I approached the girl checking tickets at the door and introduced myself as a comedian looking for stage time. She told me to go to the room behind the stage and 'ask for Werzel'. Werzel Montague is considered the elder statesman of Perth comedy and looks like Brian Blessed, if the Shakespearean actor had spent some time in the Australian bush. I explained to him that I was a stand-up comedian from Pakistan, recently relocated to Western Australia, and was eager for some stage time.

'Look, I'm happy to try you out, but you have to go through the open-mic first. This guy came by a few months back and said he was Russia's biggest stand-up, and I put him on stage and he was terrible. So I just need to make sure you're, you know, not terrible,' he said.

It seemed like a reasonable enough request and so I agreed to run the comedy gauntlet that is an open-mic. He let me into the green room, a closet space jammed tight with other comedians. Tuesdays at Lazy Susan's is when Perth comedians are given five minutes each to try out new material or hone their older material. Mixed in among the seasoned veterans are newer comics still nervously developing their craft and a few people who just want to try stand-up comedy as a bucket-list experience.

It was the first time I had ever occupied the same physical space as so many other stand-up comedians, and so I stood in a corner to observe them. Conversation was minimal, with each comic focused on whatever they would be taking to the stage. Some were writing things on their hands, other reading what they had already written there, editing it further so their palms looked like an undiagnosed dyslexic's homework assignment.

Right next to me, two guys in their early twenties were arguing over who got to keep 'the bit about sluts'. Apparently both had similar observations on the topic.

'I did it first, man,' said one comic. 'I did it here four weeks ago.'

'Yeah, but I did it at Laugh Resort five weeks ago. You can ask [names of some other comedians who could be consulted as witnesses], they saw it and will back me up.'

'Okay, I'll check with them, but more people would have seen me do it here than saw you do it there, which means my bit is more famous now.'

I was ecstatic listening to this debate over the intellectual property rights of a 'bit about sluts'. It was exactly the kind of interaction I had heard successful comedians talk about in podcast interviews for so many years when they related stories of open-mic rooms. If it hadn't occurred so naturally, I might have thought it was scripted – that every open-mic comedy night in the world is contractually required to have two comics in their green room arguing over who gets ownership of the blazingly inventive comedy on the nature of sluts.

A few minutes later, the MC called out my name and I stepped through the connecting door, walking out onto the stage. The spotlight punched me in the eyes and I could barely see beyond the front row. The audience clapped politely as I pulled the microphone out of the stand, took a deep breath and launched into five minutes of stand-up comedy.

It went well. I was worried my accent might be too impenetrable, or they might be too confused by the sight of a Pakistani standing on stage and talking about the sociocultural implications of his genitalia to laugh. But they laughed at all the same places the audiences in Karachi used to laugh, and then it was over. Five minutes done, I thanked them, thanked Werzel and drove back to Mehreen and Ali's house.

After almost a decade as a comedian, I had finally performed in an actual stand-up comedy club, in front of an audience experienced in watching stand-up comedy, and I hadn't died or been booed off. It was probably just the post-performance endorphins, but I felt like Australia might work out after all.

30

I did two more shows before we had to leave Perth. I had emailed all the comedy rooms in Perth with a short description of my credentials and comedy experience, addressing the fact that a Pakistani stand-up comedian might not seem like a guarantee of comedic skill but I had international reviews to confirm my competence.

One of the bookers responded right away, asking if I had any experiencing MC-ing. I replied that I had MC-ed a few award shows in Pakistan and he offered me a paying gig. I would have to drive out to a golf course on the outskirts of Perth and host a fundraiser for a children's ice-hockey team. In return, he'd pay me $350. He just needed to see my act once before he could confirm the job.

So I drove down to the Charles Hotel, where the booker, Johnny McAllister, hosted a weekly comedy show. The exterior of the hotel has all the charm of the hotel in which *The Shining* was filmed and I drove past it twice before realising the depressing-looking place with the ghostly twin girls beckoning me from the lobby was probably it. Inside is a cavernous hall that seats over 150 people at dining tables focused on an elevated stage.

Johnny is a British expat who has been in Australia just long enough for his cockney accent to pick up Aussie inflections and thus become completely incomprehensible. Using a combination of sign language and nodding, he communicated to me that I was required to do fifteen minutes on stage in front of the packed room. By then I had come up with a few opening bits addressing why a Pakistani was doing stand-up comedy, which I hoped provided enough context for me to jump into my older stuff. Johnny liked my act and confirmed that I could host the fundraiser the next day.

The fundraiser was exactly how fundraisers are around the world. Two boys from a suburb needed money to go abroad for an ice-hockey symposium (or whatever the term is for international gatherings of the ice-hockey world). To pay for their tickets and equipment, their family had arranged a paid event, attended by friends and neighbours. There was to be dinner, a raffle draw, an award for the largest donation and after-dinner entertainment, in the form of three comedians doing twenty minutes each and me MC-ing the entire thing. It was held in a fluorescent-lit ballroom, with tables arranged in long boarding-school dining-hall rows. The audience got progressively drunker as the evening wore on. All in all, it was a terrible place to do comedy. But comedians will perform any place they are paid to, since they are rarely paid to perform at all. And so there we were.

I survived the evening thanks to Xavier Susai, a Perth comic who had spent almost as much time as I had in the trenches of stand-up comedy. Xavier spends a great deal of time travelling outside Australia, doing gigs in Singapore, Malaysia, Hong Kong and even China. When I met him he was trying to become the first international comedian to perform in North Korea. Taking pity on this slightly lost Pakistani newcomer, he gave me advice on where to get more gigs and how to make them pay; he became the first friend I made in Australia.

A day later, at the end of our second week in Perth, Ishma was offered a job. The position was as a counsellor at some immigration detention centre in a place called Northam, and she could start immediately. Googling 'Northam' took me to the Wikipedia entry of a town an hour and a half from Perth, with a population of 6580, according to the 2011 census.

'More people worked in my office building in Karachi,' I pointed out.

'We can't really afford to be picky,' Ishma replied.

The next day we drove up the Great Eastern Highway to Northam. It was still winter and from May to September the route is lined with thick forest. As the road climbs up through the hills, it offers views of sun-dappled trees, vast meadows dotted with sheep and other postcard-ready scenes of pastoral beauty that can only be described in clichés. Appreciation of those vistas was interrupted by Anya's chronic carsickness; she vomited in what would become the first of many such gastric expulsions.

We stopped for brunch in the town of Bakers Hill, which, true to its name, has a large bakery. There I ate my first meat pie, establishing a ritual that I still indulge in on a weekly basis, despite the havoc it is probably wreaking on my cholesterol levels. Finally – after oohing and aahing over the wondrous cloud formations, flocks of sheep, grazing horses and distant hills blanketed in Crayola-yellow fields of mustard flowers – we reached Northam.

The town sits in a valley; to approach it, you take an exit road bleeding off from the main highway. A mile before Northam begins sits the Yongah Hill Immigration Detention Centre. A modified army training camp, it is a giant megalith of grey concrete with electrified barbed-wire fences and security guard posts. Inside, several hundred asylum seekers are housed under high-security conditions. Yongah Hill is so large that at night its lights outshine the lights of Northam – the whole complex glows electric-white, like a crashed alien mothership.

'That's going to be my office,' Ishma said as we drove past it.

'Cheerful place,' I replied.

We crossed a short bridge spanning a river, and then turned onto Fitzgerald Street, the main artery on which all of Northam's shops are gathered.

'Oh God,' I said. 'It's really damn tiny.'

'I feel like we're in the Shire and Bilbo will be standing on the roadside,' Ishma said.

'Not unless he wants to score some crystal meth.'

One of my Google searches had revealed that, until a few months before, a crystal-meth empire had been run out of a house here. Despite its idyllic beauty, the town promised to have a Stephen King-esque underbelly. Still, it was beautiful.

In summer everything around Northam is burned to a blackened crisp by the unrelenting Australian heat and the whole town simmers like the surface of a barbeque. But in winter the river swells, swans paddle across it with stately grace, and the surrounding hills are a quilted patchwork of thick grass and wheat fields, making the entire place the essence of rural charm. Which was, for a pair of city dwellers like Ishma and me, utterly frightening. We were Homo Urbanus. Our lungs had evolved to convert toxic levels of carbon monoxide into nutrients; the frantic sounds of traffic jams were our lullabies; and we couldn't possibly survive someplace where cheap Thai food wasn't available at midnight. Northam's air was so clean that the entire town stood out in high-definition clarity; it was so quiet that, if you burped, the police would issue a ticket for noise violation; and everything went to sleep at 5 pm. We had thought Perth was quiet and, when we considered Mandurah a possibility, I worried it might be too quaint. Northam was where 1950s England went to lie down and it hadn't yet woken up.

We drove around the town, going as slow as possible so as not to crash into the aged residents hobbling across the roads, and completed our circuit in a few minutes. Parts of Northam are still recovering from some previous collapse of industry, with factory buildings lying hollow on the outskirts; in the centre is an abandoned hospital, with broken windows and its approach overgrown with weeds. There is a Woolworths and a Coles and, as the petrol-station attendant informed us, 'A Maccas! Which means we're practically a Super Town now.' There was no sarcasm in his voice, and so I kept incredulity out of my smile.

We met with a real-estate agent, who showed us a few houses, and decided on one that seemed both affordable and easy to maintain. Built in the 1920s, but recently refurbished, it had four bedrooms, one bathroom, a modern(ish) kitchen and patches of lawn at the front and back. The porch offered a view of a milk collection plant and there was a lemon tree in the back, next to the outhouse.

We didn't know enough to ask for a house with insulation and I had never operated a fireplace, so for the first few days in Northam we almost froze solid. Despite the stereotype of Australia being slightly warmer than the surface of the sun, the temperature in Northam dips just below zero degrees Celsius on winter nights and every morning the car windscreen would be glazed with ice. We wore more sweaters and jackets inside the house than when we went out and I bought three different heaters to cook us while we slept.

Ishma started work right away, leaving early in the morning and returning at 4.30 in the afternoon after a day of counselling refugees at the detention centre. Meanwhile, Anya and I began assembling the Ikea furniture we had purchased in Perth. Bundled in several layers of wool and cotton, I fumbled my way through chairs, sofas, a bed, a dining table and a cupboard. Anya stood next to me with a toy hammer, helpfully tapping things after I was done and declaring, 'Good work, Daddy. You are a good furniturerer.'

We quickly established a routine, with Ishma returning from work every day to find me exhausted from battling the accumulation of dust, cooking food and playing with Anya. It wasn't a role I'd ever imagined for myself – that of the efficient househusband – but I adapted to it with only a little bit of kicking and screaming. Most days I would take Anya to the park in the centre of the town, a sloping stretch of grass attached to a children's play area with the usual swings, slides and stuff-to-climb-on.

Next to the park, spanned by a suspension bridge connecting the two halves of the town, is the Avon River. Some days we would take bread down there with us, breaking it into small pieces which we tossed at the ducks squatting on the bank. This became increasingly stressful because of the aggressive seagulls that swooped down, snatching the bread while it was still arcing through the air. The ducks and swans, cheated out of the snacks intended for them, began to circle us, squawking angrily as they tried to grab the bread even before it left our fingers. Eventually we just tossed the whole loaf on the ground and beat a retreat.

Before we left Karachi, all our friends had warned us, 'There's snakes and spiders everywhere in Australia, man, and they're all deadly. Be careful.' I remember replying, 'I'm from Karachi. There's suicide bombers here. Unless the spider comes up to me and explodes, I think I'll be okay.'

That bravado lasted right up until the first time I saw a hunstman spider. Walking out onto the porch one morning, with Anya still asleep inside, I lit a cigarette, exhaled smoke into the dawn sky and looked down. At my feet was the face-hugging creature from Ridley

Scott's *Alien*, covered in brown fur. I shrieked manfully and ran inside the house.

'Well, we're never leaving the house again,' I thought. 'Might as well start rationing what's in the fridge until we die of starvation a few weeks from now.'

Okay, even though the huntsman is as big as a large hand, with long brown legs and pincers that could lift a baby, it does happen to be harmless to humans. But I only found that out months later, when I related my experience to friends in town and they all mocked me.

After the initial shock of my first encounter, I decided I hadn't come all the way to rural Western Australia to be defeated by a furry arachnid. So I found a large broom, and snuck out the back door. I circled around to the front porch, stealthily approaching the huntsman from behind. With a primal yell, I brought the broom down on the beast with all my strength.

Thinking it must be jelly after hearing a meaty thud, I lifted the broom. The huntsman was still standing exactly as it had been. Then, to my horror, it turned around to look at me. 'Is that all you got?' it seemed to say.

With another scream, I used my minimal cricket skills and swung the broom like a croquet mallet. This time I connected with the spider, sending it hurtling through the sky, cutting a spider-shaped path through the pollen drifts. I'm still proud of myself for not having purchased a return ticket to Karachi for all three of us that day.

--------- • ---------

During breaks from my domestic tasks, I searched for any jobs in town I could do. There was a weekly local newspaper, so I approached and asked if they needed a reporter. 'We already have one,' they replied. Which meant I had to wait until that guy either quit or died.

It turned out that a former news producer with extensive experience in advertising didn't have much value in a town of farmers and tradesmen.

Once or twice a week I was offered a reprieve, driving down to Perth to perform in open-mic comedy rooms, hoping to prove to the bookers that I could be trusted with paying gigs. Johnny McAllister began letting me do fifteen-minute spots at his hotel venue, and at a brewery in Fremantle he also managed. The booker in charge of Lazy Susan's – a comedian named Laura Davis – also offered me a support spot in her line-up once every few weeks.

I would do the hour-and-a-half drive down to Perth, jump up on stage and perform fifteen minutes of comedy, then drive back. The money I earned was barely enough to cover the cost of the petrol, but those first few months of gigs gave me enough of a sense of purpose to stave off depression.

I wasn't ungrateful for all we had achieved in such a short amount of time. I had friends in Canada who spent a year living entirely off their savings, with no job prospects. Ishma had found work in just a couple of weeks and we were already working towards shaving days off the two-year regional requirement on our visa.

But I was jobless. After spending a decade in the institutionalising routine of high-pressure industries, I was spending every day dusting, cleaning, cooking and playing with a three-year-old girl. There is a serene joy in spending time with one's child, time that I had previously been denied due to my long work hours. We ran around the park, fed the ducks, played with dolls and built Lego towers. But those charming moments are offset by the mind-crushing boredom admitted to by only truly honest parents. It's the reason why so many housewives have a slightly crazed look in their eyes when they meet other adults, lurching into conversation like starved zombies attacking a brain buffet. You can only read *The Cat in the Hat* so many times before feeling murderous rage towards Dr Seuss and his whimsical fucking rhymes.

Ishma claims I had started eating entirely too much Nutella and begun to lose the ability to converse above a three-year-old level. None of this was helped by the complete absence of recreational activities in Northam – anything that didn't involve sitting in the pub and drinking away the pain. There were no bookstores or cinemas in less than an hour's drive in any direction, and you can only marvel at the wondrous sunsets so many times before wishing the celestial body came with a plotline – perhaps some conflicting relationships with the other stars.

31

Australians are obsessed with 'boat people'. Despite being a nation built by refugees who arrived on the isolated continent on an armada of flotation devices, in recent years the national discourse has taken a decidedly unsympathetic approach to others hoping to achieve the same feat. Every time I turned on the news, politicians were raging at the invasion of Australian shores by leaky boats filled with desperate refugees. Despite Northam being far from the coastline, its townspeople were engaged in this national problem because the detention centre had been built on its outskirts. When it was opened for refugee processing, many people in town were enraged, demanding to know why their lives were being put at risk.

During the town council meeting when the detention centre was announced, one man with missing teeth and a mullet raged into the microphone, 'If one of those people escapes, they're going to steal my car, they're going to attack my wife and they're going to drive down to Perth to blend in with their kind.' Northam residents, like the rest of the country, had been whipped into a state of hysteria by the continued insistence by politicians that 'boat people' were not to be trusted and that Australians had reasons to fear them.

Even though I'd flown to Australia on a valid work visa, I couldn't help but be sympathetic towards those attempting to reach the country by boat. Many of them came from Pakistan, and many of those were Shias persecuted for their belief by the Taliban and by an indifferent government; their families had been killed, their jobs taken from them and they faced the very real risk of being extinguished by brutal violence. They had escaped from Pakistan to neighbouring countries, which were just as intolerant of their existence. Then, with diminishing options for survival, they had paid people smugglers to take them on boats to Australia, which had previously signed the UN Refugee Convention (apparently only because all the cool countries had been doing it, and you got a free key ring and baseball cap).

Australians' insistence that arriving by boat is illegal, even though there is no law to this effect, shows that they don't appreciate how many years it takes to receive a simple work visa, even when all the required paperwork is completed in a timely fashion. Refugees who tried to gain entry through the formal process were looking at a wait of more than a decade. And it was not as though there were that many attempting to come. Australian politicians seemed to be describing a horizon blackened by an armada of boats, whereas in truth hardly any of the world's millions of refugees chose Australia as their destination.

Ishma worked with these new arrivals in her job; although she honoured the non-disclosure agreement she had been made to sign, her frustration at the ignorance of most Australians towards people desperate for safety was taking a toll on her as well. Every day she would come home looking defeated, her exhaustion blending with rage.

'Boat people' were vilified in the public discourse as threats to national safety, every one supposedly a potential terrorist. The rhetoric which began to escalate under Prime Minister Kevin Rudd – who had returned to power in a coup, which as a Pakistani I almost respected – peaked when Tony Abbott was elected. He called the refugees 'queue jumpers' as though there were orderly lines of patient asylum seekers forming outside the borders of Australia. Perhaps it never occurred to him that if those lines did indeed exist, they would be forming in the ocean and the people in them would have to be standing on boats, since Australia is an island. The Abbott government's hatred of asylum seekers was brought to the fore by the shockingly cruel tactics of Scott Morrison, the immigration minister. Shortly after his appointment, Morrison militarised Australia's protection against the scourge of desperate refugees, sending many of them back to be killed by their persecutors. Those he couldn't return right away he exiled to offshore detention centres in Nauru and on Manus Island, criticised by the United Nations as being little more than tent cities devoid of basic resources. When confronted with pleas to his sense of humanity, Scott Morrison responded with a justification based so utterly on principles of efficiency that it isn't hard to imagine that in a different time and place, he would be the man who took pride in sending the trains off full and having them return empty, on time, every time.

Angry over the treatment of people whom, in slightly altered circumstances, I could have been one of, I did the only thing I knew how to do – I talked about it as a comedian.

The first time I commented publicly on the issue of boat people, it was on stage at a comedy club. I was just trying to articulate how ridiculous I found the reaction, and attempting to explain exactly who these refugees were. I quoted the man who had been so worried about his car and wife, and then tried to convey the truth about the boat people.

'These are the good guys,' I said, 'escaping shitty countries where the bad guys won. It's not as though if Seal Team Six hadn't killed Osama bin Laden he'd be in Bakers Hill stealing meat pies. It's not a concern. These people risking their lives to get here by boat, they're doctors and lawyers and teachers and dentists. So when the man screamed, "What if they escape? What am I supposed to do?" I thought, "I don't know – invite them in. They might teach you how to read and fix your fucking teeth.'"

The first time I did that joke, I expected the audience to heckle me with all the clichéd xenophobia their elected officials kept parroting on TV. Instead, the room laughed and applauded. Emboldened, I continued.

Eventually I developed over twenty minutes of material in which I attempted to debunk the insulting myths around boat people and refugees and tried to show how the political leaders were outright lying in an attempt to frighten voters. I performed it in bars in Perth and Fremantle, a comedy club in the remote mining town of Kalgoorlie and even in the beach town of Geraldton, a week after a refugee-laden boat washed up on the shore there, giving locals a fright. Each time, I was met with agreement, shown by applause.

Australians, I realised, were being done a disservice by their political representatives. Once the inhumanity of the government's propaganda was explained to them, they responded with compassion. Despite my fears, not once did anyone heckle me or tell me to get out of the country if I didn't like it. People can always surprise you, even when it is *you* who is setting out to surprise *them*.

It was this part of my act that was eventually quoted by *The West Australian* Sunday paper, published under the headline A PAKISTANI MIGRANT WALKS INTO TOWN on the very day I decided to test the flight capabilities of my tiny car. The one quibble I have with the reporter who interviewed me after watching my show is that she didn't clearly differentiate between what I said on stage and what I said over the phone.

'If you're worried that someone who spent two weeks on a boat, lost half his family on the trip over, then spent two years in Nauru and can't speak the language can take your job away from you, then be better at your fucking job,' when appended with 'he said on stage to laughter' makes me sound less sociopathic than when it ends with a simple 'he said'.

I didn't help things by exaggerating my feelings towards Northam for comedic effect, describing it as a 'social and cultural black hole'.

When I got home from the car crash, I woke Ishma and told her what had happened, assuring her that I was fine, though we were lacking any conveyance until I got the insurance sorted.

'Oh and my interview came out in the newspaper,' I told her. 'Grab it in the morning if you get a chance.' Then I showered the crushed glass out of my hair and ears, and went to sleep.

The next morning Ishma went for her pre-dawn run. Making her way down to the petrol station, she bought a copy of the newspaper and held it up to everyone in the store, proudly proclaiming, 'My husband is in this!'

'We'll read it for sure!' said the cheery woman behind the counter. Then Ishma ran home, spread it out on the breakfast table and began to read it herself.

'They're going to chase us out of town!' she lamented when I woke up and read it as well. Less than a year after arriving, I had insulted Northam and attacked Australian governmental policy in print. My photograph over the interview destroyed my last shred of anonymity.

For the next few days, we worried about the reaction. From friends we heard that the people of Northam were incensed and my mailbox would be flooded with people contesting my views on refugee policies and pointing out that grateful immigrants should be quiet immigrants. That I could expect the same mix of cursing and threats of violence I hadn't received for a long time – not since I stopped writing my weekly columns in Pakistan.

I wondered if anyone would attack us physically and if Anya was safe at school. But when I shared these fears with one of our local friends, he just laughed and said, 'This is Australia, mate. When we get angry, we grumble over a few beers and then go home. No one's going to attack you guys.'

And no one did. A few people glared when they saw me at the grocery store, but that was the extent of the reaction. The only person ever to talk to me about it was an old man who caught up to me outside the local post office.

'Are you that Pakistani fella that said Northam had no culture?' he snarled. I couldn't help noticing that, despite his age, his knuckles looked flat and hard.

'Yes, but . . .' I began.

'Well good on ya! I've lived here my entire life and Northam is a shithole!' he said. Then he walked off, laughing to himself.

There is a sense of humour inherent in the Australian psyche; it's not as cynical as the Pakistani one, but it's just as willing to laugh at itself.

32

The day after the interview in which I tried to alienate all of Australia was printed, I received a phone call from a woman who said she was the producer for ABC-TV's *Australian Story*.

'I thought the article was really interesting. So why are you in Australia? And do you really do comedy from Northam?' she asked.

Over an hour, with Anya interrupting every few minutes to show me how much of her breakfast she had successfully dropped on the floor, I described my life in Pakistan and coming to Australia.

'Well, I'll still have to talk to my bosses, but we would like to do an episode on you. Does that sound possible?'

'I'll have to check with my wife,' I said. 'Her work involves an NDA. Plus, y'know, I'm not sure you have enough for a full episode. At most, my life will be ten minutes of "he started doing comedy in Pakistan and became moderately successful at it, although he never stopped being broke".'

'You check with her and I'll get back to you with my bosses' response in a few days,' she said.

I mentioned this conversation to Mandy, one of our closest friends in Northam. We had met Mandy and her husband, Mick, at a children's birthday party and they had helped us integrate into the town. When my car attempted violent suicide, it was Mandy who had driven out in the middle of the night to get me. When we moved to a new house – we had left the first one five minutes after a neighbour killed a venomous snake that was over a metre long in our front garden – Mick had carried most of the furniture that my skinny arms couldn't lift.

'That's a big deal,' Mandy said. '*Australian Story* is huge. We love watching it. Everyone does. You should definitely say yes.'

So we did. We never fully understood what was being offered, nor what it would entail; it just seemed like some extra publicity for my stand-up comedy. The producer scheduled the arrival of the film crew to coincide with my upcoming Perth Comedy Festival show.

An annual event, the festival was organised by Jo Marsh, a veteran of the comedy industry. I had emailed her, requesting a spot on the month-long festival program, and she had offered me one night on which I could perform an hour-long show. By then I had just begun to work as a headliner in the local clubs, driving to Perth up to four times a week.

When the festival was still two months away, we travelled to Karachi for an unscheduled holiday. We hadn't intended on returning home before a full year had passed in Australia, but a relative of Ishma's was ill and her family asked us to come. I had committed to a run of shows in the Perth Fringe Festival (held before the comedy festival and differentiated from it by featuring more burlesque acts than comedy), performing with a Perth comedian. So that I wouldn't have to cancel my shows, Ishma flew out a week before I did.

Anya stayed with me, giving Ishma time to focus on her relative's recovery, and the two of us moved down to Mehreen and Ali's house in Perth for that week, so I wouldn't have to worry about finding a babysitter for Anya in the evenings when I had my shows. During the day, I entertained her by taking her back to the zoo and visiting the Perth aquarium. On the seafront, the aquarium offered a chance to view sharks swimming around a glass tunnel through which patrons walked, thus becoming the reverse of a sushi train. In the evening, once she was asleep, I'd perform to Fringe attendees. The show was small and mostly went unnoticed by critics and judges, even though we sold out all five nights. Once it was over, Anya and I flew back to Karachi to join Ishma.

We hadn't been away long enough for homesickness to fully develop. Even so, I was quite excited by the chance to meet up with friends and spend time with my parents. But all that positivity vanished the moment the plane landed. The crowded immigration counter, the apocalyptic cacophony of traffic and the perpetual stink of exhaust all gave me a migraine I realised I hadn't had in months. It's easy to forget how good you feel until that feeling goes away. In a short time, we had acclimatised to the serenity of Northam; having that yanked away damaged my nervous system.

The day after we arrived, two bomb blasts in Quetta killed over a hundred Shias, and a friend was robbed on the way to my house. The aggression and fear I had left behind when we emigrated abroad instantly returned as did anger: anger at how people were being killed, anger at how their deaths were being justified by a nation suffering extreme cognitive dissonance, and anger at being powerless to stop it all. I was walking around with clenched fists again, wanting to find someone I could fight. I felt a desire to hurt others as a way of processing my anger.

I was experiencing the same emotions that had made me stop writing my column shortly before we left Karachi eight months before. At that time I had realised my columns were becoming increasingly less funny, with the satire and sarcasm being replaced by bitter rage. So I had stopped sending the columns as soon as I had written them, instead waiting a day to reread them and take out all the intentionally malicious things I had put in just to provoke a reaction – because every day that hunger for a reaction was growing stronger. I had gone online and written provocative things – attacking religion, patriotism and political beliefs – so that the people who tacitly endorsed the Islamic extremists, by voting for politicians who lionised the terrorists, would react to my baiting and I could use my verbal skills to punch them in their souls.

But when I had first arrived in Australia, I stopped reading Pakistani news, just so I could gain emotional distance and no longer feel the anger I was so tired of experiencing. Coming back to Karachi now, even just for two weeks, brought all of this back to me.

Of course, I also spent a great deal of time eating all the food I had missed and buying knock-off designer clothing for a fraction of the price. For the first time in our lives, the financial conversion rates were in our favour and we indulged ourselves without worry, making up for the penny-pinching we had to do back in Northam. Anya bounced between her maternal and paternal grandparents, her every want indulged with such gluttonous abandon that we had to spend several weeks deprogramming her on our return, teaching her that chocolate would not magically appear every time she asked for it. Then we all flew back to Perth.

The *Australian Story* team arrived in Northam a few days after our return. For a full week we were shadowed by Belinda Hawkins, a seasoned journalist, and Mark Farnell, a cameraman. They filmed our daily life, from dropping Anya at school to Ishma coming home from work. I cooked for the cameras, did the laundry for the cameras and even Skyped with my parents for the cameras. When I had a gig in Perth, they accompanied me, much to the amusement of the other comedians. Belinda interviewed Ishma and me separately, spending almost six hours listening to us detail every moment of our lives for the camera. It was a strange experience, regurgitating in a single sitting so much of what you remember.

It left me surprisingly exhausted, my voice worn down to a rasp. The final night of filming was at my comedy festival show, where I presented an autobiographical journey detailing my decision to move to Australia with (what I hoped were) amusing anecdotes and observations. Then, with several days' worth of footage, Belinda and Mark returned to Melbourne to begin the process of editing it all down into a coherent half-hour episode.

Being filmed for *Australian Story* was the closest I have ever come to being on reality TV. It's hard to act normally in front of a camera, and I could never forget it was there. It was made much easier by how thoroughly professional Belinda and Mark were. When, at the end of each day, the cameras were turned off, we got along wonderfully; and when they finally left, Anya was heartbroken. Even Ishma and I wished we could spend more time with them, without the constant filming. It was fun to hang out with people as news-addicted as we are, who shared our urban cynicism.

Our episode of *Australian Story* aired a few weeks later. In the weeks leading up to it, I had been awarded 'Best Local Act' at the Perth Comedy Festival, the first tangible evidence I'd ever had that all those years of stand-up comedy hadn't been just delusional self-confidence. Belinda was thrilled because it provided a nice epilogue to the whole story she was telling of a Pakistani journalist-turned-comedian and his family, who had moved to Australia hoping for a better future.

Mick and Mandy invited us to watch the show at the pub with some friends of theirs, but we declined. We didn't know what to expect and were just praying I hadn't again said anything stupid that would get us run out of town. Whenever panic hit us, we repeated the only mantra that we found effective: 'Have faith in Belinda. In Belinda we trust.'

Australian Story: Northam Exposure aired in Melbourne and Sydney two hours before the West Australian broadcast. As we walked back from dinner at the local Chinese restaurant, my Twitter feed began clogging with heartwarming greetings from across Australia. Hundreds of well-wishers sent messages of welcome in 140 characters. We rushed home and I opened my email to find more messages accumulated there. The tone of each one was the same: 'Welcome to Australia! We're glad to have you.'

A week later, I was still receiving several hundred emails, tweets and Facebook messages. In town, people stopped us in the street to hug us, welcoming us to Northam and offering help if we ever needed it. When we went down to Perth that weekend, we were asked for our autographs. I endeavoured to reply to each item of correspondence, feeling that not to do so would be rude to people who were being so sincerely and overwhelmingly hospitable. I was used to cynicism, but was instead faced with generosity and sincerity.

Pakistan's polarised environment is filled with polemics and bitter rhetoric. Its citizens have suffered so many betrayals that they find themselves unable to trust any achievement or to cheer any success. When Sharmeen Obaid-Chinoy won Pakistan its first Oscar (for Best Documentary Short), critics raced to belittle her achievement. On a much, much, much smaller scale, when I announced having won an award at the Perth Comedy Festival, the first Pakistani response was: 'Australia must be desperate for comedy.' I wasn't even surprised at that.

Malala, the young girl who has become a symbol of female rights and education, was shot in the face by terrorists who took credit for the attack. She has since spoken at the United Nations General

Assembly and been rightly awarded almost every possible honour the world has to offer. In Pakistan there are debates about whether she is a CIA spy, and claims that she is making a fuss over nothing.

That was the reaction I was used to. Instead, we received nothing but cheer and good will. Even now, six months later, I get a couple of emails a week from people who saw the episode. Somehow, with editing, Belinda had made me seem less like a narcissistic sociopath and more like a compassionate human being with a story to tell.

I'm still not sure how she did it.

33

I hadn't felt nervous about a comedy show in a while. I shouldn't at all, not after doing this for so long, but on this night the stakes were different. I was going to do my first show in Northam. If it went badly, I'd have to spend the next year in a town that not only disliked me but also found me unfunny. The latter worried me more than the former.

The show was Peter's idea. Peter Roe *is* Northam. His family has lived on the same farm just outside the town for four generations, with one ancestor being the first surveyor general of Western Australia. There's a street named after him in almost every city in the state, which is why Peter gets quite incensed whenever receptionists in town misspell his name.

Even though our daughters go to school together, we didn't meet until he called me up after *Australian Story* aired. 'Look, I figure it's about time someone welcomed you to the town properly. Why don't you come on down to my farm and we can have a drink together,' he said.

So, overcoming my natural antisocial tendencies, I drove over a few days later. The farm, it turns out, was several thousand acres of wheat and canola spread across hills and flatland as far as the horizon. Like an island in the centre of the ocean of yellow and gold was Peter's house, attended by a flock of obese sheep. Peter took me on a drive across his farm, laughing at my wide-eyed amazement at the sheer size of it. Despite being from completely separate worlds, we got along surprisingly well and he even promised to give me a ride on his combine harvester when the harvest season began. When, a few weeks later, my car broke down on the day I was supposed to speak at a writers' festival in a neighbouring town, he even loaned me a ute. The festival organisers were thoroughly amused at the sight of a Pakistani pulling up in a mud-splashed farm vehicle. So of course, when he asked if I would be willing to help the local golf club's fundraising efforts by putting on a show, I agreed.

Partly because I wanted to put on a great comedy show, and partly so that if my set went badly people might not hate me so much, I conscripted a famous musical-comedy trio from Perth called Suns of Fred to perform with me. Peter and I then printed up posters and he began to sell tickets. There was some resistance, naturally, with a few proud residents refusing to support anything involving 'that fella that slagged off Northam'. We aimed to sell a hundred tickets, figuring if we sold that many the night would be a success.

An hour before the show started, Peter called me up. 'We've sold 160 tickets. Now it's on you, man!'

'Will you do the stuff about Northam?' Ishma asked as we drove up to the show.

'I think so,' I said. 'They deserve to hear what all the fuss was about, right?'

And so, inordinately nervous despite having done this comedy thing for close to a decade, I got up on stage in front of a room full of townsfolk and began making fun of Northam. Thankfully, they laughed. They laughed at all the right places and some of the wrong ones too, which is even better. In the end, once the applause had finished, I said, 'There, that wasn't so bad was it?' Then I invited Suns of Fred onto the stage and went outside for a victory smoke.

That show felt good. Better than any other show I had done until then, because for the first time it felt like I was trying to make peace through comedy. And to an extent, it worked. From then on, the town was neatly divided in half. On one side were people who had attended the show and others they had told about it; they liked me. On the other side were people who were still angry with me for mocking Northam and would never get over it. Pleasing some of the people some of the time is all I ever really aspire to anyway, so I counted it as a win.

34

I'm writing this final chapter of the book in November 2013, sitting on the sofa in the living room with the laptop resting on my lap, where it is probably irradiating my sperm. It's just before midnight and Ishma and Anya are asleep. Summers here are torturous; with cloudless skies, the sun burns your skin and leaves skin cancers on any surface not basted in sunblock. At night, however, the wind screams across the valley in which Northam sits like a dollop of suburbs in a spoonful of farmland.

Australian Story changed a lot for us. Ishma, Anya and I are recognised by everyone in town now and the smiles we get are always friendly. The show also pumped my comedy career with steroids, elevating me to constant headliner status in Perth's clubs. I've also spoken at several refugee advocacy forums since then, becoming a miniscule part of the national debate that escalated in volume during the recent election.

Sometimes I worry that if Tony Abbott finds out that I describe him as an early-model Terminator, created when the technology was still unable to convincingly graft human skin on the robotic exoskeleton underneath, he might revoke our visa and send us back to Pakistan. I should probably stop making fun of the Prime Minister and spending so much of my time on stage railing against his anti-refugee policies, but it has become a compulsion. The louder the Australian government gets in its efforts to punish people desperate for sanctuary, the angrier my comedy grows in retaliation.

I have work tomorrow. Actual sitting-at-a-day-job-style work. It only took me a year and a half to find gainful employment in town. I am now in charge of marketing for a Northam-based company that makes steel sheds. It wasn't the job I had been hoping to get, but despite the hundreds of dollars a year earned through comedy, we were still a single-income household dependent on Ishma. So I kept plugging away at jobs advertised online, mostly hoping to find something that would take the burden off her.

I applied for this job expecting the same rejection I had received from everywhere else. They called me the next day, mostly just excited by the fact that their office is located two lanes away from my house. During the phone interview, they asked me if I had any problem working for 'a Brethren-owned company'.

'Not at all,' I said.

After the interview was over, I googled 'Brethren'. It turns out I would be working for a Christian cult that ate their meals separately and didn't socialise with people outside the community. Still, I figured, how bad could it be?

The next day, when I went in to sign the employment letter, I was anticipating the standard job-interview questions like, 'Where do you see yourself in ten years?' and 'What's your greatest weakness?' Instead, my employer asked me, 'Are you a believer?'

I was too taken aback to stop my brain from kicking into idiot-comedy-mode and replied, 'No, but I am a Belieber.' There were a few moments of awkward silence in which I realised the Brethren don't know who Justin Bieber is, which is really the best advertisement for their religion if they are looking for new converts.

Other than eating lunch at my desk, the job is going well enough. I work part-time so that I can be there to pick up Anya from school every day and in the evenings still drive to Perth for shows. Ishma still has her job at the detention centre despite my offer to pick up the burden of financial responsibility. My theory is she hasn't quit because she's worried about descending into the same fits of Nutella-scoffing boredom that marked my first months in Northam as a househusband.

A little over one year down and just one more to go. Then we can apply for permanent residency and, a year after that, citizenship. Maybe, once we've fulfilled the constraints of our visa, we can fulfil our original goal and move to Melbourne.

Sometimes, that hope keeps us sane. Northam is beautiful and the people have been kind to us in every way, but there are days when the isolation and tedium can be maddening. There are days when it feels like being locked in a container made of wheat.

It's also taking me a great deal longer to acclimatise to that brand of racism peculiar to rural West Australians. I hadn't experienced it at all until starting the job, since prior to that almost all my interactions had been with other comedians. By and large, stand-up comics are well-read and intelligent people with a sensitivity to what should and shouldn't be said out loud. Our livelihood depends on that distinction, after all. But normal people here have no such thoughtfulness. Casual racism is the social lubricant of the West Australian workplace it seems. In the last few days, I have heard every possible slur against Indigenous people, many of the words used being of the kind that I had thought only existed in movies re-enacting the worst days of American slavery. Even in those films, the actors always looked justifiably uncomfortable saying the words that a lot of people here just let slip in casual conversation. There is also the daily barrage of

Muslim jokes, which the speakers seem to find as hilarious as they are unimaginative. At first I was astonished by some of the racism that white Australians seem to think it's okay to voice, as long as it's done with a larrikin grin, and let it slip by without comment. But then I felt angry at being forced into a situation where I was being made complicit in bigotry out of my need to be polite.

One day, a co-worker saw me taking my lunch out of a bag. 'Is that curry?' he smirked. (It was lasagne.)

'Oh, that's funny,' I said, not bothering to hide my irritation. 'Because I'm brown and brown people only eat curry. Very clever.' Then I pointed at his lunch and said, 'Is that a dick?'

It seems to have worked. Since then he hasn't said anything to me that didn't involve work.

Yesterday, restless with boredom, I wondered what our lives would be like if we were still in Pakistan. An hour after I had that thought, a suicide bomber exploded in a Shia neighbourhood in Karachi. On Facebook and Twitter, Pakistanis alternated between condemning the attack and fighting with one another over the viability of continued negotiations with the perpetrators. Many blamed the Shias for making themselves such a visible target by not conforming to majority belief. Reading it all gives me the same old thudding migraine of rage, so I stopped. From Pakistan to Australia, the narrative is depressingly the same: the persecuted are to be blamed for their persecution.

But I had my answer. If we had stayed, I'd still be working in a job I detest, still writing columns that were basically attempts to create a fist with words and still doing comedy once a month at a corporate event. Ishma would be working as a psychologist and Anya would be attending school, and whenever they were away from me, I'd be fighting off panic for their safety. It's not worth dwelling on, so I'm learning not to do it. Things are different here. There are some aspects of Australia that infuriate me and others that just make me uncomfortable, but at least my wife and daughter are safe here, and that's all that matters really.

A few days back, I was in Perth on some errands and had an idea for a new stand-up bit. In Karachi I would have written it down and then waited until my next hour-long show to try it out on stage. Sometimes that wait was several months long. This time, I drove around to a comedy club nearby and asked the room manager if I could get five minutes of stage time. He's booked me several times for headlining spots and so trusts me enough that it wasn't a problem.

I jumped up on stage, tried out the new material, discovered what parts worked and what didn't and got a few laughs. Afterwards, I laughed and smoked with a few other comedians whom I've become friends with and then drove back to Northam. In a few weeks, it should be polished up enough to make it into my regular act. Doing that – getting the drop-in spot and having the freedom to experiment with my stand-up – makes me feel like I'm finally a real stand-up comedian, honing his craft the way stand-up comedians have always done. It feels good. It feels like belonging.

ACKNOWLEDGEMENTS

It's weird spending your life wanting to write a book and then finally managing to do so. There have been a lot of misfires and false starts along the way and this would have been one of them too if it hadn't been for Richard Walsh. Open up any good book published in Australia in the last few years and Richard's name will be the first to be honoured in the acknowledgements. He has a passion for the written word, a history of fighting for its dignity and a childlike joy in discovering new voices that is inspiring. This book was his idea and he took the time to convince me to write it. So thank you, Richard.

None of this would have happened without Belinda Hawkins, who made the introduction, put in a good word and starting this whole thing by telling my story with such sensitivity and acuity. She and her wonderful team at ABC-TV's *Australian Story* will always be welcome in our house and our lives.

Once Richard was done patching this mess together, he handed it over to Jane Palfreyman and the wonderful folks at Allen & Unwin. It is an honour to be represented by their imprint. Go out and buy their books, folks, and tell them I sent you when you do. It's unlikely to get you a discount though.

Thank you to Sara Amjad and Mahvesh Murad, who read everything I try to write and patiently tell me when I get it wrong. And eternal gratitude to the globe-spanning members of the Syndicate, who keep telling me to do it right. One more cup of tea, one more game of Dungeons & Dragons.

How do I adequately thank my family? Even trying to do so belittles what I owe them. Mommy, Daddy, Safu and Azmat – everything good in me is you. Thank you for letting me do whatever I wanted and telling me to stop doing whatever I shouldn't.

And finally, always, there is Ishma. When I said I didn't think this book was worth writing, she convinced me otherwise. When I wrote the first draft she told me why it wasn't working. She worked while I wrote and read when I was done. Thank you, *jaan*, for all of this. Oh, and it's your turn to put Anya to bed.